Rough Breaks

Also by Laurie Wagner Buyer

MEMOIR
When I Came West
Spring's Edge: A Ranch Wife's Chronicles

FICTION
Side Canyons

POETRY AND CHAPBOOKS
Reluctant Traveler
Accidental Voices
Cinch Up Your Saddle
Infinite Possibilities: A Haiku Journal
Across the High Divide
Red Colt Canyon
Glass-Eyed Paint in the Rain
Braintanning Buckskin: A Lesson for Beginners
Blue Heron

Rough Breaks

A Wyoming High Country Memoir

Laurie Wagner Buyer

UNIVERSITY OF OKLAHOMA PRESS : NORMAN

Publication of this book is made possible through the generosity of Edith Kinney Gaylord.

Except where noted, all photographs in this volume were taken by Laurie Wagner Buyer and are now part of the Buyer Family Collection and used by permission.

Library of Congress Cataloging-in-Publication Data

Buyer, Laurie Wagner, 1954–
    Rough Breaks : a Wyoming high country memoir / Laurie Wagner Buyer.
        pages cm
    ISBN 978-0-8061-4375-0 (pbk. : alk. paper)   1. Buyer, Laurie Wagner, 1954-—Homes and haunts—Wyoming. 2. Poets, American—20th century—Biography. 3. Ranch life—Wyoming—Biography. I. Title.
    PS3552.U8944Z46 2013
    811'.54—dc23
    [B]   2012046991

The paper in this book meets the guidelines for permanence and durability of the Committee on Production Guidelines for Book Longevity of the Council on Library Resources, Inc. ∞

1 2 3 4 5 6 7 8 9 10

For Mick
A man who loved the land most of all

And for his family: Margie, Johnny, and Melody

"... when you love a person and a place long enough you learn her secrets ..."

—Steve Earle

Rough Breaks

Rough Breaks

A cardinal calls, repeating her fluted notes in a rehearsed pattern. I open my eyes. She perches high on a delicate twig, one barely big enough to support her weight at the top of the reddish-gray plum tree outside my window. In a cupped crook of thin limbs sits an empty nest of tightly woven sticks and dried grasses. The winter wind roughs up her dull feathers. She shakes and waits, calls once more. The brighter male appears, darting across the sky like a tiny Christmas-colored kite, and settles on the nearby stone wall.

The mated pair have returned to their humble abode, one that has remained intact through months of drought, 110 degree heat, fierce winds that whipped up wildfires, and pounding bouts of prayed-for rain. With avian tenacity they have survived the tests of time and weather here in my current home, the hill country of Texas, a landscape where snow rarely makes an appearance.

I close my eyes to listen more deeply. Wind chimes on the porch next door tinkle angelic notes. Not far off, someone mows still-green grass. Beyond that, I think I hear the Llano River, but that must be my imagination, since the wide stream pours over a man-made dam a half-mile away.

Maybe, though, it is another river I hear. The Green. In the high country of Wyoming. Far away, deep down in memory, buried beneath a burden of ice and snow, of struggle against hidden obstacles, lies the miracle of release when spring comes. The log cabin I once called home a half-mile from the Green is now gone, but just as the cardinals built their nest in the safety of the plum tree, I hired on at a Wyoming cattle ranch with the hope that I would find shelter from storms and be safe from predators. What were the chances that a girl raised on Air Force bases and in midwestern suburbs might make it as a ranch hand? Slim to none, but since no one had warned me about hardheaded agricultural attitudes, environmental warfare, or the difficulty of loving a man twenty-three years my senior, I attempted to build a warm home on shifting drifts of snow.

How are we ever supposed to know whether the people and places we come to love will heal us or harm us?

Thirty years ago, when I was twenty-eight, I sulked in front of a frost-rimmed window in a playhouse-size log cabin on the O Bar Y Ranch. First light had coated the bare smoke-stained panes with silver satin. I created a mental note to sew some curtains. I had left the last ones, made from flour-sack dishtowels, tacked to rough-board frames in a cabin up at Snook Moore's ranch on Tosi Creek, where I had lived from 1981 to 1982. The big picture windows at the Flying A, a lodge upcountry from the O Bar Y, where I had spent the previous winter, had not needed drapes because there were no neighbors for miles.

I pushed up from the metal-framed single bed with its sagging mattress and tiptoed across the cold plank floor to the refrigerator to get a pair of socks and a clean shirt. Yesterday's dirty jeans over my long johns would have to do. How funny that my new abode on the O Bar Y had an ancient refrigerator but no electricity. Maybe I could move the musty Frigidaire out to the storage shed by sliding the bulky beast on a piece of cardboard, but first I needed a dresser for my clothes. I cussed myself, using an array of despicable words learned from spending eight years in the wilderness with a Vietnam vet turned mountain man. I had forgotten my mud-caked boots outside the door, and now they would be frozen stiff. Though the feed store calendar on the wall next to the handcrafted pine table under the window said June 1983, the high country had not yet relinquished winter's demeanor. Snow still clung to the deep ravines on the Sawtooth Mountains and the Wind River Range, the creeks only now beginning to rise with spring melt, and the roads in and out of the ranch barely passable.

A pair of resident skunks roused to my footsteps over their heads and began to fuss. Piteous mews escalated to more intense cries. I crumpled several pages of the Pinedale Roundup *with a couple from the* Livestock Journal *and built a fire with just enough kindling and dried pine slabs to take off the chill of the room and thaw out my boots. A crescendo of screams accompanied by a stomach-wrenching odor seeped up through the uneven floorboards from an earthy burrow. Were the skunks mating or trying to kill each other?*

"Cool it!" I said and stomped my foot like an agitated mare. I closed the stove door on the roar of flames and opened the cabin door to a welcome burst of fresh, frigid air. A swirl of returning swallows accompanied dawn's lemon-colored light. Soon the swift, acrobatic birds would begin collecting mud to daub under the eaves to build nests. A chortling chorus of sandhill cranes sounded farther away, down along the curving channel near the first bridge built across the historic Green River.

I shrugged on my chore coat, then kneaded one boot at a time in the warmth rising from the stove. Over at the main house, my new boss, Margie Buyer, would be worrying about how she would be able to pay me a monthly wage, while her husband, Mick, would be pacing the length of the living room, looking out the big windows, anxious to get going. The older blue pickup waited in the front yard, loaded with spools of barbed wire, coils of splice wire, stretchers, pliers, staples, a posthole digger, and a heavy iron tamping bar. Before he could turn out the cattle for the summer, Mick had twenty-two miles of fence to fix, and I had hired on to help.

What had made me think that I had the strength to take on such a job? The thirty-four moves of my military childhood and young adulthood had taken their toll, as had the hand-to-mouth existence I had lived with that mountain man, William F. Atkinson, who called himself "Makwi Witco," Crazy Wolf. At age twenty, when I had come west to live with Bill, I longed to be married and have children, to settle down, to be in one place for the rest of my life, to have one man to love. I wanted some degree of emotional and financial security, along with the surety of belonging that could come with staying in the same place long enough to know the calls of the birds, the tracks of the animals, the names of the wildflowers, and the shifts of the seasons.

Why hadn't I been smart enough to know that the idea of being a cowgirl on the O Bar Y was as naïve and foolish as the dream of the Garden of Eden paradise that I had wished for with Bill on the Northfork of the Flathead River in Montana? And had I learned nothing in the fourteen schools I had attended in the Philippines, North Dakota, Arkansas, Texas, Hawaii, and Illinois, not to mention the trio of years I spent at a private liberal arts college outside Chicago, and a degree in English completed at Montana State University?

Yes, I had realized that I could never return to an 8-to-5 job, or live on a military base or in a city or a suburb or even a small town. I needed the land—wide expanses of open space—to survive, and the Buyers ran Hereford-cross cattle on 11,000 acres of deeded and public lease land north of Cora, Wyoming, a town with a post office and a population of three. When they offered me the job, I jumped at the chance to learn about cattle and horses, grass and sky. If nothing else, I would have a paying job for the summer and the hope of saving enough money to buy a much-longed-for gelding.

So I traded handmade buckskin pants and moccasins for Wranglers and boots, wilderness for agrarian life, homesteading for ranching, mountain man for cowman, and I prayed that when the smoke cleared and the dust settled, I would have found a way to remain on the land.

It would not be so. In the end, I became a turncoat to an earlier hard-won lifestyle—eschewing beef and elk in favor of vegetarianism, no longer voting Republican, wearing a western hat and cowboy boots only when a special occasion calls for them. Yet my worn low-cantle saddle, split-eared bridle, and tarnished spurs still sit on a stand in a corner of the room, all that I have left of the years when I rode the high country of Wyoming, searching for a home in the rough breaks of the heart of nowhere.

Mule Secrets

On a bright, cold early winter morning in 1982, I snowshoed four miles from the Flying A Ranch on Little Twin Creek to see my new neighbor, Mick Buyer, on his O Bar Y Ranch. With my notebook and camera in hand, I joined Mick to accompany him on his livestock-feeding rounds and interview him for *Western Horseman* magazine. Though he owned a matched pair of Clydesdale geldings and two teams of black Percherons, Mick had added a brace of draft mules to his herd. They presented him with a new challenge in the face of his daily routine because working with mules was not the same as working with horses. Standing over sixteen hands, coal black with white stockings, the mules, Tom and Molly, minced around the corral and played hard to catch. Mick's patience paid off, and he tied them in separate barn stalls for their ration of grain. The mules tap-danced on the plank floor and tossed their heads.

"Nervous," Mick said, "because a stranger is here." I stood out of the way and listened as Mick told me the secrets to working with mules. "First, you have to accept a mule's basic nature and work with it. Second, you have to think like a mule in order to be one step ahead of it. Third, never trust a mule and never turn your back on a mule. Fourth, the old 'two-by-four between the eyes' routine for getting a mule's attention is not sound stock management. Fifth, mules love treats like alfalfa cubes, and a little bribing goes a long way."

Mick harnessed while Tom and Molly stayed busy with their grain. When he bridled Molly, he tied her up very short and crooned in her ear, "Miss Molly, will you marry me?"

Before she knew it, the bit was in her mouth and the headstall behind her long and touchy ears. Tom was given the same considerate treatment, the pair was hooked together, and Mick drove them out of the barn to the sled.

While we glided on top of the packed-snow road to the hay lot, Mick told me about the time Tom jumped a six-pole fence, grabbed a newborn calf by the neck, and tossed it ten feet in the air. He then lunged after the frantic cow but changed his course of action to attack Mick's son, who had tried to intervene. Johnny escaped through the deep snow, and Mick finally ran down the errant mule.

"Most mules have a mixed-up mother instinct," Mick said. "They'll attack and sometimes kill anything small—in other words, mules do not mix well with calves, colts, or kids." The calf died, and Tom spent a day in hobbles until Mick could add more poles to the fence. "Some people told me I should get rid of these 'good-for-nothing' mules, but it wasn't the mule's fault. He was only doing something that came natural to him. Might as well blame me for not building the fence high enough."

Feeding the cattle looked like a complicated venture. I had worked on a big livestock outfit, the IX Ranch, during the summer of 1980. There, in the wind-scoured breaks of the Bear Paw Mountains, I had learned to ride well enough to help gather cattle, but I had never done more than feed and milk a recalcitrant Jersey cow named Penny. Up at the Moore ranch, I had jumped at the chance to help Snook with the daily round of chores on his

quarter-section of land. While Bill holed up in our borrowed
cabin to tan hides or carve elk ivory, Snook and I hitched Nugget
and Bally, loaded the sled with some hay from the crib, forked it
out to his herd of seventeen palomino horses, fed a pair of rangy
milk cows, split wood, hauled water, shoveled snow off rooftops,
parceled out kitchen scraps for the chickens, and chopped frozen
beaver carcasses for his trio of faithful dogs. Snook had taught me
the value of getting by on what we had, to pace myself when
working in the high-altitude air, to avoid the sullen fight-prone
moose that skulked in the willows, and how to keep worry away
by humming a happy tune. But a huge difference existed between
Snook's 160-acre homestead place and the enormous workload of
the O Bar Y's hundreds of cattle and thousands of acres.

With keen interest, I soaked up the details of Mick's fine-tuned
operation. His leather-gloved hands were in constant motion as
he guided the mules through numerous gates, alongside sixteen-
foot-high haystacks, and around several large corrals in which
heifers, pairs, bulls, yearlings, saddle horses, and teams were
separated. He held the lines in one hand and cut and held baling
twine in the other. He kicked hay off the sled as he moved
through the stock, eyeballing the cattle and saying, "That steer's
got the brisket disease; that black-baldy heifer's pretty springy—
she'll calve tonight; that calf's got the scours." His eyes, shadowed
from the snow glare by dark glasses, looked everywhere, searching for any ailing animal.

When we stopped at the barn to check on a heavy heifer, Mick
used a double-sure method of making certain that the mules
stood still while he was off the sled. He tightened and wrapped
the long lines on the sled's center brace; then he snugged down a
special "mule brake"—a rope that ran from Tom's halter to the
sled's side brace. Then he tied Molly's halter rope to a fence pole.

"It's easier to use a bit of caution now," he said, "than to spend
all afternoon repairing the sled."

The huge log barn, bedded thick with wild grass hay, was
warm. A red-necked heifer's still-damp baby was up and sucking

when we stepped inside. Mick put the pair in a pole pen, glanced out to check on the mules, then forked the heifer some hay. When we returned to the sled, the mules both pawed the ground, restless to move on. Mick gave them each an alfalfa cube with his sing-song words of praise: "Aren't you the best mules ever made!"

On the way to the Black Butte feedground, two miles from the main ranch, Mick eased up on the lines and allowed Tom and Molly to stretch out into a trot. The sled pulled smoothly behind their long-legged, sure-footed gait. Day after day of travel had packed the sled trail as evenly as a graded road.

"It's not always this easy to travel," Mick said. "More often than not midwinter, heavy new snow and bad winds wipe out the trail, and though they can pull some deep snow, I try to save them by keeping the road plowed open."

The elk were nowhere to be seen when we approached the large fenced haystacks beneath the thickly timbered ridges of Black Butte. Mick pulled the mules alongside a stack, put on the mule brake, and began to load bales.

"I feed forty-eight bales a day to the 450 head of elk that winter here," he said. "I make two trips with twenty-four bales around the feedground. That helps save the mules as well." As he finished stacking the first load of hay, the elk began to appear from the groves of leafless aspen that flanked the butte.

One by one, single file, the elk trooped down the mountain-side, some trotting with their heads thrown back, some hanging behind with caution. The cows and calves, golden with pale ivory rumps, strung out along the feed line, jostling for position. The bulls were the last to come out of the timber for their share of the fine green hay.

The elk, like the mules, acted nervous with a stranger around. As long as I remained on the sled, they moved around grabbing mouthfuls of hay, watching with curiosity while they chewed. The moment I stepped down onto the snow's crust to snap photos, they broke and fled like frightened rabbits. Mick laughed and gave me a hand up on the sled again.

"They're spooky," he said. "It's strange how they learn to trust only one person. The first five years I fed here, I never saw an elk. Now they know me and accept me. Routine, doing things the same slow and certain way each day, builds trust and confidence. Like the mules, the elk have their own nature. I accept and respect that."

As we pulled away from the feedground, the elk returned to their feed. Mick's hands played the lines with certainty, keeping the mules on a steady homebound course. "See how nice and gentle they are," he said. "You just have to know how to handle them."

Would Mick harbor that much patience for a greenhorn, hard-headed young woman who desperately needed a job that paid cash? At fifty-two, alone on his ranch, Mick looked like a man who could use a hand with the chores.

Mickle-Nickle

Not long after I rode with Mick on the mule-drawn feed sled, I met him in his yard as he came in from doing morning chores. The words I had been drumming up the courage to say on my long snowshoe trek down off the mountain from the Flying A tumbled out of my mouth in a breathless rush: "What would you think about my coming to work for you?" He picked up the broom on the porch and swept the snow off his chaps and over-shoes, then stomped his feet.

"Come in," he said. He dropped his snow-crusted leather gloves on the floor grate of the oil furnace to dry and stood over the rising heat to warm his hands. Moisture from his melting mustache dropped and sizzled. He tugged at the clumps of frozen condensation and let them fall.

"Margie asked me before she left for Arizona if I wanted to come one day a week," I said. "Clean house. Do laundry. Make some casseroles. Bake cookies. Maybe help with feeding. She thought you could use some help."

"She's always trying to get me to hire someone."

"What I don't know, you can teach me. Ask Snook Moore. I helped him on his ranch last winter."

"I know. Heard about that. What about your mountain man? What will he say?"

"He doesn't get a vote. I need a job. I need some money."

"I'll think on it." He sighed. "Another day, another nickel. Your mail is on the table. I managed to make it out to the highway yesterday afternoon."

"You sure don't earn much for your hard work on this place, Mickle-Nickle," I teased.

"A nickel's better than nothing. Maybe we can figure out how to scrape together a couple pennies for you, too, Gallantry Gail." Mick flopped down in his recliner looking like a tossed-aside ragdoll.

"How did you know my middle name?" I perched on the edge of the couch.

"Written right there on that envelope in your hand. So you're a college gal?"

The way he said "college" made me sit back. "Yes, is that a problem?"

"Not if you know what the letters after your name mean."

"You mean BS, MS, and PhD?"

"Yep. Bullshit. More shit. And pile it higher and deeper."

I laughed. "Now you're being silly."

A chuckle hid behind Mick's blue eyes, but the set of his jaw indicated that he wasn't kidding.

"Don't worry. I have a BA . . . and don't tell me that stands for big ass!"

"Stand up and turn around so I can check," he said.

"No way! Why do they call you Mickey? That's not your real name."

"John Robert. Dad was John Henry. Pop was John David. Gram was Minnie. Mom said that when Gram saw my big ears and red face when I was born, she said, 'Oh, what a little Mickey Mouse.' We had too many Johns around, so the men called Dad Bill, and Mom started calling me Mickey."

"Did you mind? Growing up, I mean. Did the other kids tease you?"

"Didn't care what the hell they called me as long as they didn't call me late to dinner."

The dog quartet—Tammy, Sam, Bandit, and Tigger—set up a yowling chorus from the bay window where they had been on guard. Mick pushed himself up from his chair and opened the door to let them out. He picked up the binoculars on the counter and glassed the willow-choked creek bottom. "Coyote . . . make that two."

He limped into the kitchen, mixed himself a glass of instant iced tea, and asked me if I wanted some.

I shook my head no. Some imperceptible change came over Mick. His eyes softened; he let down his guard and told me his story.

Mick had lived his whole life in Fairplay, Colorado, going between the old homestead house near Beaver Creek, the small house in town, the three-room schoolhouse, and his Gram and Pop's big white house up on the hill. He never got to go anywhere else except to Denver with his folks to see the stock show in the years when the roads were passable. He also spent time in a Denver hospital when he was "sicker than a pup shittin' peach pits." The local doctor had come by the house, but he had been "drunker than a skunk." He poked around on Mick before he staggered out the door, saying, "If I had a pill, I'd give you one." Young as he was, Mick said he didn't trust "the son-of-a-bitch." His dad's sister had died at age nineteen when the doctor had mistakenly poured acid into her infected ear. Mick's parents and grandparents treated him "like a china doll" for the year that a ruptured appendix kept him out of school. Mick didn't mind staying home even though the illness put him behind in his class. He never caught up again, but he liked to joke that he was "the smartest one in the dumb class." In his teens, rather than hanging around town, he preferred being off in the woods by himself, or helping his Uncle Art at the filling station do some "maniac-ing," Mick's humorous play on the skill it took to be a mechanic. Mick's

innate shyness kept him from going on dates, but it didn't keep
him from having to go into the service at nineteen, when "the
Army got me for three years." After that, he had a chance to work
for the Texas Highway Patrol, but his dad wanted him to come
home. Mick never had a chance to go to college or pursue any
other career. Like his father and grandfather before him, he
"married up to a bunch of cows" on the place the family had
homesteaded in 1870.

In 1964, when he was thirty-three, Mick left the Fairplay
ranch. He said that he wanted to find a different place, one with
better water rights at a lower elevation. He was "sick of wrestling
with the big-city buyout of the water rights and the goddamned
tourists," none of whom knew how to close a gate, though they
sure knew how to open them—or cut the fences. Mick's dad
supported him by saying, "The family has been in one place
too damn long anyway."

When Mick, Margie, and his parents found the O Bar Y, Mick
fell in love with the isolated ranch on the Green River, but it made
Margie nervous. Mick confessed that the place had "eaten his
lunch" and been "a confidence chewer," because there was never
much break from the work, and he couldn't ever keep any help for
long. The only thing that was constant was the mortgage, which
was "a hell of a note." Still, he had stayed, toughing it out for
nearly twenty years. It troubled him that he couldn't keep Margie
settled, that she was "as unpredictable as the weather," and all she
wanted to do now was "hobnob down in Arizona." His son,
Johnny, didn't want to stay, either. Mick couldn't blame him; ever
since he was a kid, Johnny had wanted to be a pilot, "all the time
watching the planes fly over longing to be somewhere else."
Mick's daughter, Melody, had wanted to stay, but Margie took
her to Arizona anyway.

Seeing his family leave had been hard. Mick had sat on a
stalled tractor with a broken-down baler in the middle of
thousands of acres of hay that still needed to be cut, baled,

and stacked, and watched them go. All he had had left was his
old cow dog, Tammy.

The kids and Margie came back to help him during the summers,
and Margie always stayed "long enough to get the cattle check."
She had tried repeatedly to get Mick to come south and get out of
the snow and cold. He said he had tried the previous year. He had
sold his "whole damn cowherd" to the Bar E Bar Ranch just before
calving and had promised Margie he would "come down to the
hellhole" after fall shipping. But when he gathered the yearlings in
September, he kept back twenty-two heifers just in case.

He said, "The boss was not happy when I told her. 'Hell,' I said,
'I have to feed all this hay I put up to something.'"

"You call Margie 'the boss?'" I laughed.

"Well, what do you call the mountain man?" Mick asked.

I refrained from giving voice to the string of not-so-nice epi-
thets that popped into my mind.

The Boss

At a barbecue on the Carneys' Bar E Bar Ranch the year before, in the summer of 1982, Margie had approached me with a ready smile. Tall, with naturally wavy shoulder-length frosted hair, a touch of bright eye shadow, and big hoop earrings, she said, "I heard about you living up there at Snook's. Where's your mountain man? Why didn't he come to the party? Are you happy that remote? Do you ever get into town? Don't you miss having girlfriends?"

Margie was as at home at a social gathering as she was in the big log ranch house that she and Mick had built together. She took me on a tour when I stopped at the O Bar Y on my way up to the Flying A the following month.

"Kids' rooms and bath here in their own part of the house," she explained. "I insisted on the big river-rock fireplace, a master bedroom suite, and an easy-to-maneuver kitchen." She pointed to the endless cabinets, a double oven, and a gas stovetop. "That's so I can still cook when the power goes off."

She leaned against the deep sinks and indicated an oversize pantry, and two freezers in addition to the refrigerator so they could keep butchered beef and creek-caught trout along with store-bought poultry and pork. At one time they had raised chickens, but the skunks and weasels kept getting them. Sheep, too, but all they did was feed the coyotes.

Pausing near a built-in desk overflowing with accounting books and paperwork, she said, "That's where I live—especially in the middle of the night when I can't sleep because I'm trying to pencil out how to keep us going."

In a separate mudroom/laundry room, she studied herself in a small mirror and dabbed on a bit of lipstick. She had fought "tooth and toenail" for the added-on room so that Mick and the hired men could take off their overshoes, hang up their coats, and wash before coming into the house.

"It seems like you have everything." I tried to keep the jealousy out of my voice.

"Everything but enough money to pay the bills. That," she laughed, "and trying not to gain any more weight!"

The following week, Mick and Margie invited me to join them on a trip to Idaho Falls to stock up on supplies for the winter. Margie drove Johnny's Trans-Am so she could stop and see a friend, while Mick took me with him in his one-ton pickup so he could load up barbed wire, baling twine, and other supplies. The three of us met up later at a place that sold roasted chicken and took our lunch down to a park along the river. We faced a horde of other fall shoppers at Ware Mart, where we piled case lots of canned fruits and vegetables, multiple packs of toilet tissue and paper towels, and twenty-five-pound sacks of flour and sugar into the shopping carts. We loaded Mick's truck "to the gills," and he took off for the ranch on his own.

The long drive home began with Margie growing silent, her look pensive. We studied the copses of aspen mixed in with the pines that created a green and gold mosaic on the hillsides. The slight hum-and-squeal of the tires hugging the curves on the winding highway through the Snake River Canyon sounded forlorn. Driving one-handed, Margie fiddled with her purse, took out a

cigarette, then changed her mind about smoking. She had been
trying to quit. Wanting to shift the awkward silence, I began asking
her the hundred-and-one questions that one woman always asks
another when they are strangers to one another's worlds.

Margie had been born Margaret Louise Yates in Colorado Springs,
where her dad was the executive director of the Chamber of
Commerce. As a girl, Margie adored the horse-drawn milk wagon
and begged the driver for rides around the block. She saved her
nickels to pay for short rides at the local stable, and even hitch-
hiked to the dairy to see the cows. During high school, she liked
to hang out at the livestock auction, while her older sister, Ruth,
and two brothers, John and Rick, acted "more citified." She
thought the name Margaret was awful, too sedate and serious, so
she nicknamed herself Margie because it sounded light-hearted
and fun-loving.

In her mid-twenties, she landed a job as secretary to the oil
magnate Cap McDaniel on the Hartsel Ranch. There she kept
records on the registered cattle and learned about bloodlines,
cow-to-pasture ratios, and Quarter horse breeding. A hand
named Jack who worked with her at the ranch invited her to go
to noon dinner at the Reverse 3 Eleven, where his wife had
taken over the cookhouse job. That's where Margie met a tall,
lean, silent young man named Mickey—on the Buyer home
place. Margie said that his combed-back hair and the hard line
where the white of his forehead met the tan of his face made him
look scared. After dinner, Jack took her horseback to show her the
old gold dredge on the river. He told her not to tie the gelding she
was riding, that he would rear back and break the rein, and the
horse did just that when Margie didn't trust that he would ground
tie. Her embarrassment increased when she and Jack met Mick
out by the shop on their return. He promptly spliced the break in
the rein using his pocketknife. She had always said that if a man
didn't carry a pocketknife, then he wasn't meant for her. Out of

the house, away from his parents, Mick warmed up, teasing Margie and joking with her. He looked pretty danged handsome wearing his black hat tipped back on his head so that he could see to work. He liked her pretty eyes, wide smile, and ready laugh. That alone was not enough to set Mick's parents' minds at ease. They warned him about marrying a woman who had been raised in town, one who had a fondness for parties. But in their late twenties, at the end of November 1959, Mick and Margie walked down the aisle of the little white chapel in Fairplay.

Mick had inherited his grandparents' big house on the hill with forty acres of pasture and balm of Gilead trees, so the newlyweds moved in there on their return from a short honeymoon in Santa Fe and Mexico. Margie wanted to raise sheep and have a couple of burros. That idea gave Mick's cattle-minded family more cause for worry, as did the fact that she spent all the money he had saved from his cattle sales to remodel the outdated kitchen. The worst of it for Margie was that Mick assumed that being married meant that they didn't have to go out anymore: no more dates, dances, parties, or going to Colorado Springs or Denver just for fun. He even locked the door and told Margie, point-blank, "No more gallivanting!" The romance of ranch life began to fade before Margie even had a chance to get used to her married name.

Twenty-four years later, Margie slowed the low-riding car to turn off the highway. We bounced over a cattle guard and onto a gravel stretch called Forty Rod Road to take the shortcut across the valley to the O Bar Y. Despite what she had shared, it surprised me when she said, "You know, Laurie, sometimes I want a divorce so badly I can taste it. I just want to be free to be myself and do the things that I want to do. I don't want to have to worry about Mickey anymore."

One More Wreck

A few weeks later, during the fall gather, Margie's horse Sonrisa slipped on icy ground and fell with her, shattering her wrist. "Son of a pooch," she said when I stopped by and found her with a cast up to her elbow. "I've had more horse wrecks and surgeries than anyone on the Upper Green. If it's not kidney stones from the well water, it's broken bones. Doc Johnston said he should give me a prize. Blast Mickey for moving us here!"

Margie made it sound like a bad thing. She thought me naïve when I said that the O Bar Y seemed like paradise despite being snowed in for months, twenty-two miles from Pinedale and hundreds of miles from my parents and family. Margie had dedicated herself to taking care of the kids, cooking three meals a day for Mick and the hired man, and keeping up with housework and yard work, bookwork and cattle work. In the early years she didn't have time to think about being lonely. The winters were horrible and the calving seasons ghastly, but get-togethers for brandings, barbecues, and fall gathers helped. The kids had Future Farmers of America, the county fair, and rodeos. Big groups kept cabin fever at bay by snowmachining all over the country, taking along flasks of blueberry brandy to stave off the cold. When I told Margie that I had never driven a snowmachine, she said, "You better learn. It's the only way you're going to get out of this place." She swore one winter that if she had to make another loaf of bread in order to keep from going crazy, she was going to go hang herself in the barn.

She grew weary of the endless snow and cold; she needed sunshine and bird song, warm weather and flowers. And she wanted to be around people. During Johnny's last two years of high school, she rented an apartment and moved the kids into town for the winter. When I said, "And left Mick alone?" She replied, "Go ahead and blame me. Everyone else has. He was plenty irked. He accused me of being 'a goddamned people lover' and said he wished he had 'stayed in San Antonio as an HP' instead of working himself into the ground on a ranch."

When Margie reached the last of her "I'm a good wife" reserves and couldn't stay one more winter in Wyoming, she tried to convince Mick to sell the O Bar Y and move south. He reluctantly accompanied her to look at places in Arizona, and she convinced him to buy the UX in Santa Clarita County in 1977. Mick, however, refused to budge on selling the O Bar Y, and he only went down to the Arizona ranch to visit once. When he saw the desert and the thin cattle, he said he couldn't face the notion of hauling his cows to that kind of country. "Damn it, I'd rather have them freeze to death than die of thirst." Furious, Margie admitted defeat. She sold the UX, but kept back some acres for herself so she would still have a place to live in Arizona.

I understood Mick's reluctance to leave the ranch he had called home for so long. I knew the fear he felt at leaving what was familiar for something foreign. Having dedicated himself heart and soul to the O Bar Y, Mick was incapable of letting go. But Margie didn't understand why Mick was never ever able to do something for her, to help her, to save her. Didn't he think that she counted for something?

Even though Margie kept the ranch records and managed the finances, picked out the replacement bulls and selected the new horses, she still felt that Mick didn't appreciate her. Even though he knew she was a good businesswoman, he liked to call her a "tightwad" because she kept the only checkbook, tracked every penny, and made sure the books balanced. She knew every vehicle and piece of equipment on the place. Maybe Mick did most of the work with the cattle, but Margie worked with the CPAs and attorneys, the title company, the bank, and the oil and gas leases.

"Margie," I said, "I think Mick does consider you important. He told me that he wouldn't have the ranch to call home except for your frugality."

"He said that? Why is it that he can talk to you and not to me?"

"There's nothing at risk with me. I'm only a sympathetic ear. You would probably get more out of Bill in an hour than I get in a month."

When Margie's dad died in 1979, he left her a small inheritance. She used the money to make a down payment on a townhouse in Green Valley, Arizona. She didn't tell Mick she was leaving until she was packed and ready to go that fall. He didn't seem too upset. He said, "Well, at least I'll still have Melody." But then Margie had to tell him that she was taking Melody with her. She "hated like the dickens" to leave him alone on the O Bar Y, but what was she supposed to do? Stay until she succumbed to complete despair?

After years of separation, still struggling to make things work, neither of them appeared bitter or mean-hearted. Because the ranch had to come first, they had to find ways to get along. Though sad and frustrated, they remembered loving one another. I was sure Mick still loved Margie, but she said, "You know, my mother used to tell me, 'If he loves you, he'll do things for you and with you.'"

My mother had suffered from a mental and emotional maladjustment called agoraphobia. I understood that kind of fear and sensed that Mick was incapable of living closer to town or around a lot of people. Margie had never heard of agoraphobia, but she said she knew about depression. She could come back for the summers to work in the hayfield and help with the fall gather, but when winter came, she had to get out of there; otherwise, when the road snowed shut, she felt like she was suffocating. I didn't understand because I loved the time of year when the roads closed and the high country became pristine again. Like a sanctuary.

"Once you live here long enough, it will start to feel like a prison," Margie said.

"I don't think so," I said.

"You'll see." She looked around. With one hand she straightened the pile of mail on the counter, separating the newspapers and magazines from the bills. "I don't care anymore. I know that sounds terrible, but it's true. This place is like an anvil around my neck. I can't even breathe anymore."

"You'll feel better once you're in Arizona."

"Right now I've got to worry about *getting back* to Arizona. And how am I going to take care of everything there with this?" She held out her casted arm like a broken wing.

"Melody will help you," I offered.

"Doubtful." Margie awkwardly poured herself a cup of coffee with her left hand. "I can't seem to keep Melody in college or out of trouble. All she wants to do is hang around with that directionless, apathetic boy. Maybe I did the wrong thing taking her down there with me. At least here she had a good group of friends, did well in school, and barrel raced."

I was certain Melody would find her way, like we all did.

Margie shook her head, making her hoop earrings dance. "She's running wild. Got a smart mouth and a snotty attitude. The last thing I need to hear from Mickey is 'I told you so.'"

Trying to be a girlfriend to Margie and a buddy to Mick wasn't smart. I had played the role of peacemaker and mediator in my own family, and with Bill and his family, but the only thing to come from those attempts had been a trampled heart.

Miss Melo

The pretty girl with sun-streaked long brown hair stood before me in the kitchen at the Flying A Ranch during the summer of 1982. Her face carried a streak of sweaty dust, and the bottoms of her jeans were muddy. Thin and as athletic as a ballet dancer, Melody had been out fixing the forest fence with her boyfriend, Terry. Not enchanted with the job, they had wandered across the meadow to meet Bill and me.

"Dad told me some mountain-man guy was living up here, and he had a woman with him," she said by way of introduction when I opened the door to find her on the back porch.

"Do you like it up here?" she asked. "I always thought it would be kind of cool to live up here."

"I like it fine. It's a treat to have electricity, refrigeration, and running water."

"Really?" she asked.

I offered her a glass of water from the faucet, which she accepted, drinking it down in one long swallow. I looked out the window to where Terry stood chatting with Bill near the woodpile. Bill stood shirtless in the sun. His broad shoulders and chest shiny with sweat, his long dark hair pulled back by a beaded headband, he leaned on the double-bitted ax stuck in the chopping block.

Melody peeked out as well. "He's handsome, but kind of old. Do you just live with him?" she asked. "You know, like not being married or anything? Do you sleep with him?"

"Well, sure," I said.

She nodded as if the notion confounded her. "I'll be glad to get off the fence detail. I bought my dad a plaque last year for Father's Day that shows an old beaten-down cowboy struggling with barbed wire and stretchers. It says 'My Dad works for the Department of De-fense.' It's funny."

The mosquitoes that summer were thick enough to carry someone off. Terry had forgotten to bring the bug spray. Melody blamed herself for running out of water. Her ancient stretchers wouldn't hold the wires right, and Terry complained a lot because he had thought his time on the O Bar Y would mean riding horses or going fishing. It was hard for Melody and her mother to come back to the ranch and "see the place falling down around Dad's ears." Two of the gates coming in were broken. There were holes in the bridge. The kitchen floor was so covered with grease from Mick frying hamburgers that Melody said she could have used it "for a skating rink." She had taken to calling the ranch "The Oh Why Bother."

Melody lingered at the table by the window with Bill's antique manual typewriter and a piece of elk ivory half-carved with the image of a howling wolf. She touched the coyote, lynx, marten, and mink pelts hanging from elk antler racks. Her hand hovered over the thick hair on a black bear hide over the back of the couch.

"Did you do the beadwork?" She examined rifle cases, possible bags, buckskin shirts, pants, and moccasins.

"That's my entertainment. That and reading."

"Don't you ever go to town? To a movie? To a dance? Bowling?"

"Just to get groceries and supplies. It's a long way in and out. Six miles through your ranch. Nine if we go out through Schwabacher's. That's a lot of gas—and a lot of gates to open."

"Well, Mom is glad you're up here. She needs a friend. She told me if I want someone to talk to when I get married, I'd better call a girlfriend. Maybe we can all go ride sometime. She and I like to come up here on the forest to check on the cattle."

I walked Melody to the door. I didn't want to tell her that after living in the mountains for eight years, I still didn't have a horse of my own.

Later, when I stopped by the O Bar Y, Margie was in town getting groceries, and Mick was out in the shop welding, but Melody was making a half-hearted attempt to clean the carpets, while at the same time fully absorbed in the TV broadcast of the movie *On Golden Pond*. We watched Henry Fonda kiss Katharine Hepburn.

"Do old people still do it?" Melody asked.

"Of course." I laughed.

"Gross!" she said. "Why would they still want to when they're all old and wrinkly?"

"Ask me that again when you're eighty," I said.

Her mom and dad had been married almost twenty-five years, and Margie slept on the couch most of the time. I told Melody that I didn't feel that close to Bill after eight years. That we had grown apart. That life kept getting in the way of love. That worries about money and kids took their toll. It wasn't easy for me to explain to her that I wasn't married and didn't have children because Bill objected to both. She wanted to know why I stayed with him. "He may be old, but he's a good kisser when he wants to be. He knows how to 'suck face,'" I said, quoting a line from the movie.

"Oh, gross again!" she said.

"I bet you'll change your mind about that."

As I helped her drag the carpet shampooer from the living room to the dining room, we talked about the problem of couples fighting all the time, as evidenced by the long-married pair in the film and her parents. I often said things to Bill that I wished I could take back once the words were out of my mouth. I had my father's temper and was not successful at controlling it. Melody felt that the argumentative part of her nature came from her mom because her dad was pretty quiet. Terry made her mad all the time; so had Johnny when they were kids. She had once taken after him with a piece of pipe, and when he locked himself in the bathroom to escape her wrath, she pounded on the door, leaving dozens of crescent-shaped marks that marred the wood.

It was unfair, Melody said, that her brother had gotten all the brains in the family. When I teased that she had gotten the beauty, she countered by saying that Johnny, with his blond hair and his father's blue eyes, was handsome, too. But she didn't miss his being on the ranch. She was glad he was gone, because "his only goal since he was a kid was to get off this ranch." He had never taken a shine to horses or cattle, but he loved anything with an engine. Trucks, snowmachines, motorcycles. When he was sixteen, Johnny had talked his dad into buying an airplane for him, a Cessna 180. When he wasn't flying, they could lease the plane to the Forest Service to help make the payments. Did she like the idea of her brother being a pilot?

Melody shrugged. "Made me nervous to stand in the yard the first time he flew over the ranch. He waggled the wings, then dove it down like he was going to crash. He's a showoff, but he's good at getting what he wants."

I helped Melody lug the canister of dirty water from the carpet cleaner out the side door, where we dumped it on the drying lawn. What did she want?

"Not to have to go back to stupid Arizona. I hate it down there, and I don't want to go back to school."

"Wouldn't it be okay for you to stay on the O Bar Y and help your dad?"

"If I did, who would Mom have to take care of her? Do you know how awful and unfair it is to have to choose between your parents?"

Learning the Ropes

In November of 1982, on one of my forays down from the Flying A to the O Bar Y, Mick came out of his shop wiping grease off his hands with an old housedress. "What's broken?" I asked.

"What's not?" He shook his head like he had heard a doomsday prediction. "I've got to haul Margie's six horses down to Arizona. You want to come and take care of the dogs and the barn cat? Feed the replacement heifers while I'm gone? Everything else can get by on pasture for a week."

I said, "Sure, no problem," but I felt anxious and knew that I was being tested.

Mick took me through the routine of throwing hay, checking gates, chopping ice off the creek waterhole. He showed me what to do if the furnace went out, and told me who to call if I had any problems. He spent a couple days plowing the road so he could get his pickup and the trailer load of horses off the ranch.

The day that Mick drove away, I stood at the bay window and watched until his truck gained the hill near the elk feedground on Black Butte and disappeared around a bend. Then I was on my

own in a silent white world. I had invited Bill to come down from
the Flying A to join me. He showed up long enough to eat the
steak and potatoes I had prepared, but he remained mostly silent.
When he untied his horse from the hitch rack in the front yard,
he said, "I'm not sure why you want to be someone else's slave
labor, but it's your deal." He rode home to the Flying A in the dark
and didn't return.

After doing the morning feeding chores, I filled those few days
with cleaning the house, baking bread and cookies to store in the
freezer, shelling pecans, and decorating the holiday tree that Mick
had cut and put in a stand before he left. At night I sat mesmerized
in front of the television, watching movies delivered via the huge
new satellite dish in the side yard. Since I had not had such entertainment in years, I easily became addicted. Besides, the sound of
other voices kept me company and prevented me from hearing
the howling wind and blowing snow.

On the day that Mick was scheduled to return, I spent countless
minutes standing at the bay window, staring out over the barren
white landscape, searching for movement or a spot of color that
would mark his truck coming home. When he finally arrived, I
couldn't wait to tell him everything that had happened with the
heifers and the dogs. And I wanted to know all about Margie
and Melody.

When my animated monologue ran down, Mick said, "You're
hired. The boss said she would pay you fifteen dollars a day, one
day a week."

I couldn't stop smiling as I set meatloaf sandwiches on the
table for Mick. I mentally calculated that by summer I could save
several hundred dollars. Before he sat down, Mick took out his
wallet and handed me a ten-dollar bill. "Here," he said. "Buy yourself a new purse. I noticed yours is falling apart."

When I hesitated, he said, "Go on. It's an early Christmas present."
I wanted to cry. No one had done anything that nice for me in a
long while.

Mick became my champion. He kept the trail between the
O Bar Y and the Flying A packed down with his Ski-doo 399, and

I marked the way with tall willow sticks so that I could find the path after a new snow. I skied or snowshoed those eight miles, depending on the weather, and on the days when I was too exhausted to go back home under my own power, he took me most of the way on his snowmachine. He always stopped in a copse of aspen trees about a quarter-mile from the Flying A lodge, and I went on the rest of the way alone and afoot. Mick knew that the mountain man wasn't happy about my working away from home, but I refused to care about Bill's feelings or the fact that he was miffed at me for choosing to be a common laborer. What I cared about was making money and helping Mick. Having a job made me feel that I had a future to look forward to.

Mick followed me around the house like a lost pup as I did laundry and cleaned, or hung around the kitchen while I concocted good things to eat. We never stopped talking to each other, never ran out of stories about our pasts to tell each other. He had a great sense of humor, teased me endlessly, and told pathetic jokes like "What do you get when you cross a turkey and a wildcat?" (A gobbling pussy.) Or the Christmas story of Santa Claus going down the chimney into people's homes to leave presents and everyone wanting Santa to stay and visit, but he would reply, "Ho, Ho, Ho, I've got to go. Got to get all the gifts to the children you know." Then Santa slid down a chimney and was welcomed by a gorgeous woman in a negligee. When she sweetly asked Santa to spend a bit of time with her, he replied, "Hey, Hey, Hey, I think I'll stay. I can't go up the chimney this-a-way." Sexual innuendo was not Mick's forte, but it was the only way he knew how to flirt or make suggestions about wanting a closer relationship. I found his awkwardness endearing—and I savored the attention.

In December, Johnny graduated at the top of his class from Embry-Riddle Aeronautical University, and when Mick drove south for the celebration, I watched the ranch once more. The whole family came home for Christmas, but I stayed secluded on the Flying A. I wrote a holiday letter to my mom, telling her how fond I had become of the Buyers. Being around them made me long for a family of my own, but that would not happen if I stayed with Bill. "What's the matter," Bill said on Christmas Eve, "didn't your friends want you around?"

I took a deep breath. "We were invited, but I declined. Did you want to go?"

"No. You think they're so magnanimous, but they're using you."

"They are paying me."

"Slave wages . . . and I haven't seen you contributing any cash up here."

"Margie said she would pay me in the spring."

He stood in the doorway with his arms crossed over his chest and snorted at me as if I were the biggest dupe in the world.

"Even if they weren't paying me, I would still go help Mick. If we had any kind of trouble, he would be here in a minute to help us out."

Bill's narrowed eyes spoke his disbelief.

"They are nice to me."

"Well, soak it up now, because it isn't going to last."

"Why are you so hateful and prejudiced?"

"Because people are famous for telling you one thing and doing something entirely different. As long as you keep volunteering to be a saint, they will keep on taking advantage of you. Just like Snook did."

"Snook never did one thing wrong."

"The hell he didn't."

"I keep trying not to be pissed off, but you make it damn near impossible. Snook gave us a roof over our heads and—"

"We built him a new root cellar and brought in extra loads of hay, and piled up a few cords of wood. Plus you worked for him every single day. Where did that get you?"

"You make me crazy."

"You *are* crazy if you keep ingratiating yourself with others because you expect them to be decent human beings in return."

If I said one more word, we would be in the middle of another full-scale verbal war, and I hated that. I had never won an argument

with the mountain man. And he had never said he was sorry—
not for anything.

When I woke the next morning, I found a pair of hand-sewn
sheepskin moccasins next to my pallet on the floor. I shrugged on
my robe and slipped my feet into the cushy-warm booties. Bill's
bed against the wall was, as usual, not made. I could hear the
woodstove popping in the other room. I floated across the cold
floors and found him at his desk, where the early sun illuminated
the carving he was working on. I waited until he finished marking
a precise line and raised the magnifiers from his eyes. I lifted the
hem of my robe and did a little dance to show off his gift.

"No one else will give you that kind of a present for your
Christmas."

My girlish joy deflated. I took the book that I had ordered for
him in its brightly wrapped paper and set it by his place at the
table. I mixed a bowl of cinnamon roll dough and set it to rise,
then traded my warm slippers for cold boots and went out to feed
the horses and goats, with Kyote the hound trailing my heels.

Contrary Moose and Ever-Present Elk

January 1983 was not particularly bad for snow depth, yet Mick and I ran into trouble. With long, wide meadows edged by three creeks—the Little Twin, Big Twin, and Mud—all flowing to the Green River, the O Bar Y was prime moose habitat. On thousands of acres, with a couple dozen haystacks to choose from, one cow and calf chose the stack that Mick and I were feeding from as their home base. On many mornings, seeing us coming with the team and sled, the cow would round up her calf and trail out. Then came the day when she refused to leave. She would not even retreat to the far side of the drifted-in stack. Instead, she stomped her feet and wagged her tongue, her calf a perfect hackles-raised mimic behind her. The anxious team of horses Jack and Jill, moose-wise and wary, chose not to advance. The cow refused to budge off the packed trail. Mick, his jaw clenched, was determined not to give in. Back and forth, back and forth, charge and retreat, until the high-strung team lathered and Mick cussed at the moose, "You goddamned old sow! Move before I go get the .30-.06."

Then the cow lunged—not to the side, but dead straight, right
up the tongue of the sled, between the two rearing horses, miraculously not striking either one or getting tangled up in the tugs or
lines. She whizzed past us over the sled, her lanky calf following
in a clatter of tiny hooves. Then they were gone.

"Jesus." I still had hold of the metal post at the front of the sled.

"That was nothing," Mick said. "The kids tried to get home
from school once in the pickup and had a standoff on the bridge.
Damned moose wouldn't give an inch. Kept charging and striking
the truck hood. Johnny had to gun the motor, lay on the horn,
and creep forward until he finally shoved her into the willows."

"Snook told me about his run-ins with them, but I never saw
anything like that." I took off my scarf and swiped at the sweat on
my forehead.

"You should have been with me horseback when a bull in the
rut followed me for miles trying to get at my horse. Had to gallop
hell-bent across the sagebrush to get away."

"Would a moose surprise-attack someone?"

"Shouldn't worry about that. The dogs and horses have built-in
moose sensors. They only need a whiff of moose before they'll
hightail it for home."

"I understand now why Jack and Jill were so terrified. Are they
going to be okay?"

The team still shook, turning constantly, ears back, to look over
their shoulders. Jill had pawed a six-inch hole in the snow.

"We've spent a lot of time in moose therapy, haven't we?" Mick
coaxed them forward toward the haystack as their legs trembled.
My heart still thudded as he murmured reassurances to his horses.

This was not the worst he had ever seen. One time Mick had
had to saw through the poles of an eight-foot fence where a cow
moose had gotten caught by her hind legs. The "damned old thing
kept lunging and chomping the air" and did not show one bit of
gratitude, because she charged Mick after she hit the ground.

Another time Mick counted twenty-two bull moose trailing
nose-to-tail out of a stack yard, but "one old bastard" refused to

leave. John Fandek, who had been helping Mick feed cattle that day, was a fine wildlife photographer, and he was trying to hold on to the horses and aim his camera at the same time. Mick decided to "chouse the bull out of there" and got off the sled. The bull came around the corner of the hay pile like a freight train, and all Mick had for protection was a snow shovel swung back over his shoulder. That and his cow dog Tammy, who rushed in with her teeth bared to defend him.

"What happened next?" I asked as I took my hay hook from the holder on the front of the sled.

"He killed me."

"You goofball!" I said. "How many bales do you want me to throw down?"

"Better take forty." He gave me a boost onto the snow-laced stack.

That afternoon, after lunch, seeing the moose on the plowed road, Mick cranked up the grader with the v-plow and shoved the cow and her calf all the way to the river. I watched from the window as they plunged off into the deep snow, made the thick ice, and trotted off in their odd, gangling gait. Mick continued on across the bridge and up the hill across the Green.

I was taking oatmeal raisin cookies out of the oven when he returned.

"Where did you go?" I set out a glass of milk for him.

"Decided to plow out the gates at the elk feedground. Another storm's coming in. You better get on home, too."

"Let me finish this first. The elk aren't as a big a problem as the moose, are they?"

"Calmer by nature and tending more toward herd mentality," Mick said, dunking a cookie. "Moose are individual rogues, but the elk have caused me no end of trouble, too, when they get into the hay."

In the early years, with five hundred cows to feed, Mick couldn't afford to lose a bale of hay. The stacks were fenced with seven strands of wire, but even that gives way when a large herd pushes all at once. One fall, after fixing the fence till he was blue in the face, Mick started calling the Game and Fish Department to come and get their elk out of his hay. In what he called "typical government fashion," they couldn't be bothered to respond.

After waiting over a week, Mick drove out to the hay meadow and opened fire with a .30-.06. He only meant to scare the elk off, but instead his one shot dropped not only a cow but also the spike standing next to her while the rest fled. He ended up spending the next hour gutting elk by the glow of the truck lights; then he hauled them home and hung the meat in the equipment shed. The next morning, two game wardens appeared on the front porch. They had seen truck tracks, blood, and what was left of the gut piles. They asked only one question: "Where are they?" Mick pointed to the shed. They went and looked, then came back and wrote him a ticket. He either had to pay a fine or appear in court and explain to the judge what had happened.

Mick refused to pay the fine. He figured the Game and Fish ought to pay for all the hay the elk had eaten or destroyed, plus all the fencing repairs. The game guys threw the evidence in the back of their truck. Mick pulled on his overshoes and coat and followed them into Pinedale. After hearing the case, the judge shook his head, pounded down the gavel, and said, "Give me twenty-five dollars in court costs and get out of here." He told the wardens, "Give that man his elk back. He might as well eat them, rather than have you take them to the dump."

The game wardens never bothered Mick after that. Instead, they gave him the job of feeding the elk at the Black Butte feedground. Mick said, "I don't get paid much, but now I manage the elk the way I want to."

"Which means what?" I brushed crumbs off the table and put Mick's glass in the sink.

"It means if you are a wise steward of the land, you give the animals enough to eat and you take care of them every day. That's how you keep the peace."

I stood at the door and struggled into my too-tight coveralls. "But you haven't made peace with the moose?"

"Not with the moose, or the beaver, or the coyotes, badgers, gophers, moles, or magpies. Not even Margie. Some things can't be done. Some things elude the peace. They're like the enemy hiding down inside us."

Captivated

On February 2nd, the anniversary of his father's birth, Mick was waiting at the front door when I skied four miles in to his ranch after hitching a ride to Jackson Hole to renew my driver's license. Exhausted, I slipped off my skis and accepted his invitation to come inside and warm up before going another four miles up to the Flying A.

I plopped down on the couch with a glass of water while Mick sat straight in his recliner, poised as if ready to bolt out the door. "What's wrong?" I asked.

"I . . . "

"Are you sick? Did something happen to Margie? To the kids?"

"I really missed you. This is so . . . well, I think I love you."

"That's fine. I love you, too." Delight and fear warred with the calm I tried to portray.

"I'm old enough to be your father."

"That's true, but we can still care about each other."

"But . . . Margie . . . and the mountain man. Geez, Gallantry, all we do is struggle."

"Mick, I'm not sure . . . I mean, I don't want to encourage you, but I don't want to lose your affection, either. Can't we keep on being friends?"

"You sound like a schoolgirl."

"Turn on TNN," I said to break the awkwardness. "Who does Ralph Emery have on today? Did you see any good music videos while I was gone?"

That evening, back home at the Flying A, I wrote the lyrics to my first song. The following Monday, after I finished helping Mick with chores, I gave the handwritten paper to him. "It's just a song," I said. "I know you want to stay married to Margie, and I want to stay with Bill."

I didn't wait for Mick to read the words. I headed out the door for the long trek back to the Flying A, where another round of chores and housework and cooking waited for me. But I couldn't keep the song's chorus from running through my mind:

∾

There's a blue-eyed cowboy calling out my name
a blue-eyed cowboy waiting to be tamed
a blue-eyed cowboy's gonna be my own best friend
a blue-eyed cowboy's gonna love me 'til the end.

∾

A few days later, after a big storm, I snowshoed a short distance through huge drifts up to a cabin above the Flying A where the absentee owners had a telephone. I had been given permission to use the phone whenever I needed to, and they had shown me where the key to the door was hidden on the porch. Something had been telling me to call Mick. When he answered the phone, he sounded surly, but when he realized who was on the line, his tone brightened.

"Where are you?"

"Max's cabin. I felt like I needed to check in on you."

"Thanks for the song," he said. "You've got a pretty good talent with words."

"What's bothering you? I can tell by your voice that something's wrong."

"Nothing really," he said. "Oh, hell. I just got off the phone with Margie, and she's badgering me again to sell out here and move down to Arizona. She doesn't get it that I don't want to leave here, no matter how tough it gets. This is my home. This is where I belong, and I'm never leaving, not for anyone. She is never going to make me sell out."

"Mick, it's okay to feel that way. All my life I've been looking for a place to belong, a place that I would never have to leave. She can't make you do anything you don't want to do. Try to help her understand that the next time you talk to her."

"That'll be like talking to a fence post. She doesn't want to hear anything I've got to say."

"But you're okay, right? I can't come down for a few days. One of the goats is getting ready to kid."

"I'm fine. I've got enough crackers and peanut butter to see me through."

On March 11th, the anniversary of Mick's father's death, another storm blew in over the Sawtooth Range. I had never seen anything like it during all my years in the mountains. I stood at the big picture window in Mick's bedroom, where I had just finished changing the sheets after taking the laundry out of the dryer. A portrait of Margie, with her beautiful smile and wide-set eyes, hung above the queen-size bed.

"Mick, come here." I walked to the bedroom door and waved at him in the living room.

He rose from his recliner, where he was watching the early evening news. We stood side by side to watch a wild wind whip the still-bare willows along the creek into a frenzy. Then silver walls of rain swept down out of a blackening sky to pound against the window, making the entire house shake.

"Good," Mick said. "This'll soften the snow crust."

Captivated, I stood shivering in my red-and-white-striped top, blue jeans, and the white tennis shoes I wore indoors. I turned to

say something to Mick, and he took me in his arms and kissed
me. Not a shy or hesitant kiss. Not a demanding kiss full of desire.
Just a short kiss that said, "Sorry, I couldn't help myself."

Giddy, I laughed and stepped away. Mick stayed where he was,
but he held his arms open. I walked back into them, and he held
me against his chest, his flannel shirt warm against my cheek.

"Don't worry," he said. "I won't do that again. Don't know what
got into me."

I wanted to say, "I do. I know that you're lonely and I'm lonely
and that we like each other, and that's okay." Instead, I remained
quiet and allowed the moments to pass as we watched the storm
shift and move, the rain turning to sleet and then to hail and then
back to rain. Mick's heart pounded slow and steady against my
ear. He felt as warm and solid as a rock in the midday sun.

We spent many March evenings watching *The Thornbirds* on
television in between going to the barn to check on the calving
heifers. "Hell of a fix for the *padre*," Mick said, "to love someone
he can't have."

"Don't you think it's just as hard for Maggie? She loves him, too."

"Oh, I don't know. She's young. She can have anything she wants."

When I came down with a horrible cold, Mick fixed me a hot
toddy by mixing hot water, whiskey, lemon juice, and honey.
Floating like a butterfly from the effects of the alcohol, I snuggled
into the bed in Melody's room. Mick came in to say goodnight.
He spoke in a whisper to tell me that a couple of years before, after
Margie had gone to Arizona, a bunch of his so-called neighbors
had left a *Playboy* centerfold open in his mailbox.

The "buck naked" photo of a "long-legged beautiful gal" did
get Mick's attention, but he laughingly said he was relieved that he
had gotten to the mailbox before the delivery lady. I asked him
whether he had ever been with anyone besides Margie. He said,
"Once with a friend who stopped by to check on me, but—" I told
him I didn't need to know who she was, but I was glad that he'd
told me. And he hadn't been with Margie for a long time. She had
told him the last time he tried that she was "too old for fooling
around." He laughed and said, "Hell, maybe I'm too old, too."

I didn't hesitate to tell Mick that Bill and I were still intimate at times, but that mostly we seemed to be angry at one another, that I couldn't seem to find the right way to be around him anymore. He said he felt the same way with Margie, like he was always going to say or do the wrong thing.

"Why does it happen like that?" I asked him. "Why do we stop loving people?"

"Maybe we haven't stopped loving them. Maybe they stopped loving us."

He squeezed my hand and patted me on the shoulder. I leaned over and kissed him lightly on the cheek. As he walked out of the room, I said, "Don't close the door all the way. It makes me less afraid."

"If you get scared, come get me. You know where I am."

The Kid

In late March, Johnny came home to stay at the ranch and help his dad. With a degree under his belt, he had agreed to fly for Sulenta Construction out of the Pinedale airport. He told his dad and me that he would be happy to go with a much smaller company like USAir, Frontier, or America West to start with, but he had his mind set on flying for United Airlines someday. When I asked him how I could help, he said, "Could you help me type up a draft of my resume? Please."

Like a typical young man, Johnny liked to sleep late and contributed daily to a seriously messy bedroom. I started calling him "The Kid." When I tired of walking across clothes and boots and books to make his bed each day, I told him I wasn't going to try and keep up with his sloppy habits.

"What do you do all night," I asked, "wrestle alligators? Your bed is always torn apart, and I didn't spend hours ironing your shirts to have you toss them on the floor. From now on, it's your job. But why don't you keep your door closed!"

Johnny smiled and said, "Sure, Miss Laur, whatever you say."

He liked it when I baked his favorite cheesecake or his mother's
sour cream chocolate cake with chocolate icing, which I served
along with huge glasses of ice-cold milk that he had a tendency
to knock over and spill. He always offered a crooked grin with
such affection when he said, "Sorry, Miss Laur," that I easily for-
gave him as I mopped up the mess. He didn't drink coffee in the
morning, but he liked bacon and eggs and toast for breakfast,
so I left his portion under the heat lamps above the stove.

Mick and I were usually done feeding by the time Johnny
wandered outside to help with chores, but he was good about
getting supplies in town or bringing in the mail. He returned one
day wearing a brand new pair of exotic boots from the Cowboy
Shop. Showing them off, he bragged to his dad that he had gotten
a good deal. They were on sale for $275.

"What?" I shouted. "You spent that much money for a pair
of boots?"

"Elephant ear, Miss Laur, they'll last forever."

"For that price, they'd better," I said.

I asked him if there was anything he'd ever wanted that he didn't
get, and he replied that he had wanted a VW Beetle, but his mom
said he couldn't have one because they weren't safe. He had to
settle for a Trans-Am and a Chevy pickup instead. He had
winked at me then because he knew as well as I did that he
was spoiled, but not spoiled rotten.

During one of the high country's common spring storms, the
snow fell heavy and the power went out, which shut down the
pump to the well. Johnny had to be in town to fly for John
Sulenta, and he was grumping around the kitchen, complaining
about living in a place where a guy couldn't even get a shower. I
had just finished hauling up two five-gallon buckets of water
from the creek about five hundred yards from the house.

"Go haul a couple more buckets of water, and we'll heat it on
the stove so you can wash up," I said.

"Are you crazy?" Johnny got on the phone, which, thank god,
was still working. He called all over the county until he found a

friend who lived where the power was still on. He grabbed a set of clothes, shouted goodbye, and roared away through the snow. At the highway, he would trade his snowmachine for his pickup and be off. I looked at Mick. He shrugged. "I can't blame him for wanting a life with more conveniences, more excitement than snow and cattle."

One evening when Mick asked Johnny to run down to the cow barn before he went to bed and check on a few heifers that were getting ready to calve, Johnny griped a bit but pulled on his overshoes and coat. Outside, he started up his truck, drove a few hundred yards down the hill, got out, left the motor running, went into the barn, came back out again, and drove back up the hill. When he entered the house, I scolded, "For goodness' sake, why did you drive when you could have easily walked that far?"

"Miss Laur, it's dark out there. And cold!"

He stretched out on the sofa with a Louis L'Amour novel and to watch a rerun of *Mayberry RFD*.

"Comfortable enough?" I teased as I brought him and his dad each a bowl of popcorn.

"Come on, I grew up without TV. All we had was the radio, eight-track tapes, and the CBs."

I jokingly said that he had the telephone, but he complained that they were on a party line, so everyone in the whole county knew what was going on if he made a call. When they got a private line, Johnny had to beg his mom to get a long enough cord for the phone that he could take it from the dining room into his parents' bedroom. Hiding in the closet was the only way he could find enough privacy to talk to his girlfriend.

In early April, Johnny rumbled into the yard with a new snowmachine. The Polaris dealer, Bucky Neeley, had gotten him a very good deal, and the new model had more power than any other machine he had ever ridden. He spent hours crisscrossing the snow-covered landscape, zooming down swales, then goosing it full bore to see how far he could make it up steep inclines. He practiced hard because he intended to win the King of the Mountain hill climb in Jackson Hole in May.

Sometimes he blazed into the Flying A to visit with Bill. He admired Bill's physical fitness and upper body strength, which the mountain man was all too happy to show off by doing muscle-ups on a high bar. Johnny also got a kick out of the fact that Bill loved to be towed behind the snowmachine on a pair of skis. No matter how fast Johnny went, even over rough country and down steep drop-offs, he couldn't throw the whooping, exhilarated Bill off balance.

One night after supper, when Johnny had gone to a snow-machine hill climb in Logan, Utah, I sat on the kitchen counter after I had finished the dishes. Mick munched on double-chocolate oatmeal-walnut cookies. Pushing aside the most recent stock paper, I said, "Don't they know the worth of wild horses? Why shouldn't the government intervene to stop their capture and slaughter?"

"Because the grazing rights the ranchers are paying for are going to animals with no value."

I told Mick that there was a value to magnificent creatures running free and wild. Marguerite Henry had proved that in *Mustang: Wild Spirit of the West,* a book that I had read when I was fourteen. Michael Martin Murphy's song "Wildfire" had also sparked my imagination with the idea of coming to the West in the first place.

"I know it's childish," I said, "but don't we all want to be unfettered like the mustangs?"

"Pretty hard to own a ranch and remain unfettered."

"I know that. But isn't it still what people yearn to do?"

Mick shifted his shoulders as if his back hurt. What did I dream of doing? Being a writer. I already was a writer; I had written about him and his mules for *Western Horseman.* But I wanted to do more. Maybe write books or go back to school for an advanced degree. Maybe teach eventually. I wanted to find a way to make a more secure future for myself.

"You have a future here," Mick said.

"Do I?" I asked. "I'm not so sure about that, but I like it that you think I do."

"We put Johnny through college; Melody, too, if she'll stick with it. We could help you, too."

"I'm not so sure that Margie would go for that," I said. "Not when she finds out about us."

Surgery

In late April, Johnny blasted into the Flying A on his snowmachine. "Can you come? Dad hurt his leg. His knee's out. I took him to see Doc Johnston in Pinedale, and they scheduled arthroscopic surgery for him at the hospital in Jackson Hole next week."

"What happened?"

"Dad said it started with that wreck on Dancer when he was moving cattle last summer. Doc said the ripped ligaments never healed and finally gave way."

"Let me pack a bag."

A week later, Johnny stayed on the ranch to take care of chores, and I rode with Mick to the hospital. I stayed in his room with him as they prepped him for surgery. He looked very pale and unsure, not anything like the strong and self-assured man I had come to know so well in the past seven months. I chattered like a magpie to keep him company, especially when I realized that he was afraid to go under anesthesia.

"I don't like the idea of some sawbones who patches up skiers carving on my knee."

"You're just uncomfortable being away from the ranch."

"It's like being in a foreign country," he whispered when a nurse came in the room. "They don't speak my language."

"I'll do my best to interpret for you and help you feel safe. Besides, the nurses like your good looks and cowboy humor."

When they finally came to wheel him away, I walked by the gurney and held his hand. Groggy with drugs, he blinked at me and licked his dry lips. He looked like a terrified little boy. I could smell his fear.

"You're okay," I said. "I'll be here when you get out, and I'll call Johnny."

I spent the hours alone in Mick's hospital room sitting in a straight-backed chair with my eyes closed and my hands folded in my lap. I prayed endlessly for a successful surgery.

What would happen to Mick if he didn't have full use of his leg? I also asked God not to let him die. I told God that I needed Mick, and then I admitted that as much as I didn't want to love him, I did. There was nothing I could do about that, even though I had no idea what would happen to either one of us, or to Margie and Bill.

That afternoon, after an uneventful surgery, Johnny came for a short visit. It surprised me when Bill walked into the room with him.

"Here." Bill laid a handmade buckskin vest on Mick's lap. "A get-well gift."

"Thanks." Mick fingered the soft leather. "Nice of you to come to the 'horse-pistol' to see me. You know what I mean? Sometimes you're better off just getting the gun instead of letting these pill-pushers have a go at you."

Later that night, when visiting hours were over, Mick wouldn't release my hand. "Listen," I reassured him, "I'm only going four blocks away to stay overnight. I'll be back in the morning before you have breakfast."

He nodded and swallowed hard, then let go.

When I drove us back to the ranch the following day, Bill was waiting at the house to welcome Mick home. I set out pastries

that we had picked up at the store in Pinedale on our way back up
the valley. The three of us sat around the big dining room table,
where the bright spring sun poured through the bay window.

"Here," Mick said, pushing the plate toward Bill, "have a tart."

"That's not a tart," Bill said. "That's a tart"—and he pointed at me.

The slur slipped over Mick's head, but the words slapped me
hard. I left the room so I wouldn't snap back at Bill, but I realized
at that moment that I would leave him, even if I didn't know how
or when. If that's what he already thought, that's how I would act.

As Mick's knee healed, Johnny and I did the best we could: a
greenhorn gal and a grouchy, grounded pilot trying to rope
pneumonia-ridden, diarrhea-filthy calves so we could poke
scour pills down their cold, raw throats. We laughed a lot to keep
from cussing. We teased each other unmercifully. We gritted our
teeth when we had to drag off the dead. Johnny said he liked it
that he could run the ranch the way he wanted to, because all his
dad could do was run around on the three-wheeler and criticize
how we were doing things. I scolded Mick like an outraged
mother when he tried to come outside to help.

"Hell of a note when a guy can't even get off the pot," he said as
I helped him on and off the toilet and assisted him with dressing
and undressing. I told him that if he would go to town for the
physical therapy Doc Johnston had ordered, he would be able to
put weight on his leg again. He replied that he was not driving all
the way into town to have some harpy nag him because he had
one right here doing a pretty good job of that. I suggested that he
do his exercises and quit bellyaching.

"You and Johnny doing okay out there?" He winced as he bent
his knee.

"I killed that crippled calf. We switched from using the feed
sled to the wagon. The sun is eating away the snow crust. Yesterday
it took me two and a half hours to get back to the Flying A. I had
to slog for four miles instead of ski."

"If I had my goddamned leg again, I could carry you up there
on my back!"

Ten days later, we had another cow and calf moose join us, this time in the ranch house yard, where every dawn they gazed in the picture window and watched us watch them. We enjoyed our close scrutiny until the cow got feisty and would not let us out the door to go feed. Mick said that we would "fix the wicked ole sister" and got out the cherry bombs. I stood aside while the guys fired barrage after barrage of the noisy explosives over the cow's head. She merely flattened her ears. Johnny suggested that the .22 would put her on the run. Mick rained a series of airborne shots that only made her duck her head.

"That does it," Mick said. "I'm going out to feed my goddamned cows!" He told me to go out the front door as a decoy, and told Johnny to get the .30-.06. "If she puts me down, shoot her."

Mick left his crutches and hobbled out the back door. I poked my head around the corner of the front porch. When the moose rushed me, hackles raised, I slammed the door in her face. Mick circled through the snowed-up pasture to the barn, only to be met in the corral by the charging cow.

Johnny levered a shell into the rifle and stepped out into the front yard. Mick managed to leap on the sled and grab the double-bitted ax. The next time the moose charged, he flat-ax smacked her upside the head. The blow broke the handle out of the ax, but only managed to daze the cow.

"Dad! Run!" Johnny shouted as Mick made a stumbling escape into the barn. We watched as Mick trudged roundabout through the deep snow to get to the shop.

We heard him crank up his 399. He came churning through the drifts, throwing rooster tails of snow into the air. The cow moose bolted. Amid much circling and expansive cussing, with Johnny and me cheering from the sidelines, Mick convinced the surly moose and her calf to turn onto the road for a fast-trotting trip downriver.

Mick returned, still cursing and holding on to his knee. "Dad," Johnny said, "you should have let me do that."

"What, and let you have all the fun? Goddamned old sow wasn't going to let me feed my cows. Guess I gave her the what-for. Bet she's got a hell of a headache."

When the road opened up, I rode into Pinedale one day with Johnny in his Trans-Am to buy groceries. I felt pretty fancy being in a souped-up car with a good-looking, smart young man. Johnny teased me by saying, "A little easier than life with the mountain man, huh?"

He didn't understand why I wanted to live that way. He didn't even understand why his dad wanted to stay and ranch in such a difficult place. Johnny wanted to be out and about, seeing all there was to see. He was like his mom that way. He didn't much like the idea that his parents weren't together, but he understood why his mom had moved to Arizona. "Relationships are never easy," I commented, grabbing hold of the door handle as Johnny rocketed down the straightaway on the ranch road and braked just in time to slide up onto the highway.

"Miss Laur," he said. "I'm glad you're here taking care of my dad. He needs somebody. I know it hurts him that Mom left and took Melody, too. I know I'm a disappointment to him because I don't want to be a rancher."

"I'm glad I'm here, too," I said. "And you need to go do what you want to do, to follow your heart. Your dad understands. He'll be okay as soon as his knee heals."

Caesarean

Going back and forth between the Flying A and the O Bar Y became a mental and an emotional balancing act, rather like walking on live coals or, better said, walking barefoot for miles in below-zero snow. When I was at home with Bill tending to goats, horses, dog, and cats, I worried about Mick and his cattle. When I was with Mick, I worried about Bill. Only while traversing the terrain in between the two ranches was I free to focus on myself. Heading downstream toward the O Bar Y filled me with joyous anticipation, while going back uphill to the Flying A filled me with dread. I yearned to tell Bill everything and try to explain to him what I was thinking and feeling. He, however, had no desire to talk—about anything. He used silence as torture and ignoring me as punishment. I adapted by schooling myself in the "I don't give a shit anymore" tradition.

Since Bill would not speak to me, I imagined what he was thinking: there she goes again, off on another infatuation, falling for someone who pays her compliments and makes her feel like she's special. When Margie comes back home, she'll set Laurie

straight and reclaim her husband. Guess who will return to me
with her tail between her legs?

As I trekked in silence, snowshoes packing a new trail or skis
swishing in sibilant ease, I did recall the many times Bill had been
good to me. He had allowed me to share his rare wilderness world.
We had relished blissful moments and passionate hours. It was
easy to remember him playing the piano for me, swimming with
me in the river, pushing me on the rope swing, or galloping around
the meadow on his Appaloosa stud with me holding myself against
his naked back. There had been firelight and lamplight, candlelight and starlight, moonlight and sunlight. He had an incredible
ability to bounce back from horrific arguments with boyish charm.
If I could erase those memories, would it be easier to leave?

Bill had taught me things that most people would never have the
opportunity to experience, not the least of which was an intimate
connection to the natural world and all its animals. I had learned
not to be afraid of the land, the night, the beasts, or being alone.
What I still feared were people—their ability to hurt and to harm.
What I still feared was my inability to understand the workings of
the human heart. In loving Bill so completely, I had injured my
essential spirit. I had given away parts of myself to try and quiet
his chimeras. In loving Snook as a girl loves a grandfather, I had
regained some semblance of myself. In loving Mick, I was dis-
covering the woman hiding inside, a late and somewhat fragile
bloomer. However, in loving Mick, I was hurting Bill, hurting
Margie, maybe hurting Mick's children and destroying his family.
Why did it have to be that way?

In mid-May, Bill skied out. He caught a ride to Rock Springs,
where he planned to catch a flight to Oklahoma to see his friend
Carol, then go on to Missouri to see our friends Len and Lisa. They
had an old International Scout for sale, which he intended to drive
back. When I asked him when he would be home, he said he didn't
know. Maybe a week, or two, or three. He was trusting me to stay
home and take care of everything, which meant that he didn't
want me going down to the O Bar Y and seeing Mick so often.

After he left, I spent most of my time with the animals, talking to them, trying to figure out what I needed to do. Worse than leaving Bill, I would be leaving all of them as well, especially Sis, the skittish new black mare, and Kyote, the bloodhound–German shepherd cross who had guarded our door for eight years.

I called Mick late one afternoon from the absentee neighbor's phone to see how he was holding up. Not good. Johnny was gone. A heifer was trying to calve, but she was in trouble, and Mick couldn't do "a goddamned thing on crutches." He had called the vet but didn't know whether Dr. Renow would get the call, and even if he did, he might not be able to get in because the crust had gone out on the snow. Johnny had called to tell his dad that he had barely gotten out to the highway. I told Mick that I would come as soon as I milked the goats and fed the horses.

I skied through the trees on mushy snow with no resistance as the sun was going down. Holding my breath, I dragged my ski poles to decrease my speed during the wild ride. I reached the open vista below Big Twin Creek and whooshed toward the Haley meadow. My arms pumped, my legs quick-swishing in time. One more mile, and I would be at the O Bar Y to help Mick.

Fully dressed, coat and all, he waited for me on the front porch. He had redesigned his crutches with ski pole bails to keep them from sinking into the snow. He strapped his crutches on the front of the three-wheeler and sat sideways on the seat to protect his healing knee. I shucked off my pack, took off my skis, and climbed on back. We jounced down to the cow barn in low gear in the near-darkness, Mick being very careful to keep the three-wheeler on the hardest part of the packed trail.

The heifer was down, worn out, barely breathing when Mick lit the lamp. No part of the calf showed from her swollen vaginal canal. Mick couldn't get down on his knees to check, so he asked me to roll up my sleeves. He handed me a tube of lubricant for my hand and told me to reach inside and see if I could feel anything.

I hesitated only a moment, thinking that if I could slip a tampon into my own body, I could just as easily slip my hand up into the

cow. The tight opening gave way to my fingers, then my whole
hand, but all I could feel was warmth and wetness. I didn't feel any
feet or anything like hooves, a hock, or a leg. I pushed farther in,
all the way up to my elbow. "Something smooth and round," I said.

"Damn. Backwards," Mick said. There was nothing more I
could do. If Mick could get down on his knees, he could cut out
the calf and save the heifer. When he said he ought to get the gun
to keep her from dying the slow way, I pulled out my arm and
wiped it on the burlap sack Mick held out to me. He saw the
tears in my eyes.

"Don't do that. Not now. Damn it, I hate being a goddamned
crippled-up old man!"

The roar of a snowmachine sounded outside, coming up fast
from the bridge. "Johnny," we both said at the same time. Mick
hobbled over to swing open the door. Coleman lamplight spilled
out onto the snow. The vet, Bert Renow, struggled off of the snowmachine, gently cussing the weather and the long, difficult drive.
"Why do you live so blasted far off the highway . . . only for you,
Mick . . . Otherwise I'd be at home enjoying my dinner. What
have you got?"

In minutes, Dr. Renow and I, with much cajoling and shoving,
got the heifer up and tied her head to the stanchion. He slipped
on a plastic glove that went all the way to his shoulder and
reached inside. He confirmed that the calf was backward, but
also that the heifer didn't have enough pelvic spring to give birth
to even a normally presented calf. Did Mick want him to do a
caesarean? Mick hated to spend the money, but he hated to lose
the heifer even more.

I stood back and watched as the vet punched anesthetic into
the cow's tail set, shaved her side, dosed her skin with iodine, took
out a scalpel, and sliced through her hide, then the fascia, then
the extended uterus, where we could see the calf moving.

"Alive!" He pulled the little bugger out and dropped him in
the hay.

Mick told me to wipe the mucus out of its eyes and nose, and to use a hay straw to tickle into the nostrils. The calf sneezed, sucked in air, and offered a blat. The heifer responded with all the maternal instinct she could muster. Dr. Renow quickly shook antibiotic powder into the wounds and stitched the cow back together in layers. When we untied her head, she turned immediately to lick her calf. "Worth saving," he said as he packed up his gear.

Dr. Renow fired up the snowmachine. He shook hands with Mick and nodded at me. Mick and I stayed to watch until the swaying headlight disappeared over the hill beyond the bridge, then climbed on the three-wheeler to go back to the house.

I started to strap on my skis to head home to the Flying A, but Mick suggested that I stay the night. But Kyote was outside, and I had not put the goats in the barn.

"They'll be all right," he said. "Come on in and get warm. We're both tired . . . and the mountain man isn't going to know one way or the other."

Kyote

At dawn, I gulped a cup of coffee thick with sugar and started back up to the Flying A. From a distance, I could see a large black object on my willow-marked trail. At first I thought of a moose, and a chill raced down my spine. No, too small. A calf. No, no way could a young calf have gotten out of the corral by the cow barn and wandered this far. A coyote. Possible, but what was it doing lying on the trail? When I got closer, moving forward with caution, I saw that the dark lump was our dog.

"Oh, girl," I thought, "what did you do?" She was old. Her legs had given out on the soft trail. Was she dead? "Kyote?" She thumped her tail. She didn't have the strength to raise her head or even whine. I knelt beside her. "It's okay. I'm here."

I tried several times to get her to stand, but she couldn't do it. My only choice was to go back to the O Bar Y and tell Mick. I caught him as he was going out the door to check on the new calf and get the feeding done, crutches and all. I told him that Kyote was flat out, that she had come all that way looking for me. Mick said, "Calm down—I'll find a way to get you both home."

We managed to hook up a Skiboose to Mick's 399 to bring
Kyote back to the O Bar Y. It took both of us to wrestle the ninety-
pound dog into the sled, but she lay quiet and still and licked my
hand. We manhandled her onto the porch, and she ate the treats
that I swiped from Mick's dogs' dishes. Then I went with Mick to
do the chores.

Later, Mick could get us only as far as the Flying A meadow—
from there on, the snow had disappeared, vanished into a shining
lake. When we stopped, Kyote shoved herself up into a shaky sitting position, then scrambled out of the sled and stumbled over to
lap up water. She quivered like a drunk with *delirium tremens*, but
she had her legs.

We could make it the rest of the way. I would go slowly on my
skis to repack the trail, and take Kyote step by step around the
meadow to the more solid road. My voice carried across the wide
expanse to the barn, and the goats set up a bleating chorus of
welcome. I begged Mick to be careful, not to reinjure his leg by
doing too much. He would be fine. He would send Johnny up to
check on me. Don't do that. I would call if I needed anything.
Was I all right? Not really, but I didn't know what to do about it.

Mick said he needed to go. I asked him to promise me one
thing. What was that? "Please promise me that no matter what
happens, you'll try to be Bill's friend. I need to know that." He
nodded agreement and snugged down his hat. I waited until I
couldn't hear the roar of his snowmachine any longer before I put
on my skis and shouldered my pack. "Come on, girl," I said to
Kyote. "One slow step at a time."

I lost track of the days. As the snowpack melted, Bill's horses
wandered, and I couldn't find them. I struggled not to call Mick,
but I finally did. He came on his three-wheeler, and I climbed on
behind with a halter and a lead rope. He didn't think that they had
gone far; they were probably restless from being cooped up all
winter and had followed the fence lines south searching for grass.

We finally found them, hours later, in a 2,200-acre pasture on
Schwabacher's Quarter Circle 5. It was nearly dark as I haltered

the Appaloosa, Wraitheon. Mick gave me a hand and boosted me
up bareback. He was worried about me, about all the miles I had
to go, but I knew that Jere and Sis would follow Wraith and me
back to the Flying A. "Call me," Mick shouted as I gigged Wraitheon
into a gallop to try and beat the fast-descending blackness.

I tried to stay at the Flying A. I tried to wait for Bill to come
home, but I couldn't. Like a petitioner waiting for a stay of execution, I paced and stewed. After a few days, I called Mick to ask
what he had been doing. Trying to get the road in shape so cattle
trucks could get in to deliver a load of yearlings. The drive shaft
on the patrol had broken, and the son-of-a-bitch was mired in a
bottomless mud hole that was blocking most of the road. He
would get it figured out. Had I heard from the mountain man?
No, but I had seen a herd of a hundred antelope. John Fandek
had called. Snook was in the hospital. His team had run away
with him, and he had broken three ribs, his shoulder blade,
and his collarbone. Who was going to take care of Snook? Doc
Johnston wasn't going to let him go home until he had some
help. Could I come down to help Mick and Johnny with the cattle
when they arrived? Okay. At dawn on the scheduled day, I locked
Kyote in the cabin and walked down to the O Bar Y. Ninety-two
head of yearlings had been delivered to the neighbor's corrals at
the Bar E Bar. Johnny and I rode over horseback, and Mick drove
his truck.

John and Lucy Fandek's kids, Susan and Aaron, helped Johnny
and me herd the tail-kinked yearlings cross-country to the O Bar Y.
When one heifer turned back, Mick hollered out his truck window,
"Let her go! We'll get her later." We lost several steers despite
cussing and kicking our horses into a flat-out gallop through the
sagebrush. Finally Mick counted eighty-seven head through the
gate at a piece of land called the Point and onto the snow-free
pasture. Moving a bunch of wild-eyed dingbat yearlings proved
to be no easy task, but surely it was easier than trying to skin out
beaver or braintan buckskin.

Mick and I spent an afternoon shoveling my old Vista Cruiser out of its winter hibernation drift near the highway. He drove it slip-sliding up the mucky road to the Flying A, with me following on his three-wheeler. I would be better off riding his old saddle horse back and forth. Surefooted and wise, Poco made our passages times of joy for me as we trotted alongside the fast-melting snow-machine trail and picked our way up through the aspen trees. Headed back down to the O Bar Y, he became a rocket of pulsing energy, eager to get back to his own pasture and his horse pals. We flew skidding up to the yard gate on a sunny afternoon and came face to front bumper with Margie's mud-splattered pickup.

My heart thrashing against my ribs, I led Poco to the barn, unsaddled, and turned him loose. Margie met me at the front door. She didn't look angry. Instead she seemed relieved, glad she had made it into the ranch, because getting through on the muck-hole road hadn't been easy. Why was the patrol still stuck in the mud? Mick was waiting for parts. I shucked off my gloves and jacket and set them on the chair by the door.

She thanked me for taking such good care of the house, and for working so hard in the yard, and out in the barns and corrals. It was nice to come home and find all the work already done. She and the kids were glad that Mick had someone to help him. Margie and I drank coffee and ate chocolate cake. Then she added up the days that I had diligently tracked. "These were all fifteen-dollar days, not seven-fifty days?" she asked.

I took a deep breath and said, "Those were all full days, and sometimes I stayed overnight to help check the heifers that were calving, but I didn't add any more time to the list for those hours."

"You stayed overnight?" She raised her perfect eyebrows.

"Yes, whenever Mick needed me to after he had his knee operated on." I paused and then added, "I slept in Melody's room."

She nodded and wrote out the check. I accepted it. Then I said the words that I had rehearsed for the past month: "Margie, I can't stay with Bill anymore. I would like to live on the O Bar Y and work for you and Mick. But if I can't do that, then I'm going to get a job in town."

She studied me for some time, but I didn't let her stare me down. My car was mud-bound up at the Flying A. Would she let me borrow a truck to go into town to open a bank account? "Take Johnny's blue one." She handed me a list and asked me to pick up some groceries at Falers and put it on her account. She would talk to Mick and see what he thought about hiring me full-time. They might not be able to afford me.

She rearranged the stack of bills on her desk and took a long sip of coffee. "And you don't need to worry about me finding out about anything. I already know. Mick called quite a while ago and told me."

What had he told her?

Spring Cleaning

By the time Bill returned from Missouri driving the beat-up but serviceable four-wheel-drive Scout, I had thoroughly cleaned every room in the Flying A lodge, mucked out the barn, built an outdoor pen for more expected baby goats, and split another small mountain of wood from the rounds that lined the south-facing wall. He pulled up in front of the door buoyant and happy. Len and Lisa were hard at work developing a new kind of saddle called an Ortho-Flex. They had all talked of going on an extended pack trip up into the Wind Rivers, maybe exploring the Sawtooth Range. Everything looked like spring was here. The snow had given way to mud. The sandhill cranes were back lower down.

I looked out the window. The lake on the meadow had soaked into the thawing ground, and the first sprigs of green grass were poking up through the previous fall's old-gold stalks.

"Critters okay?" he asked when I didn't respond to his report of his news.

"Goats are fine. Daisy's getting ready to kid. Sis is being good about the halter. I can lead her now."

"We'll have her under saddle by summer," Bill said, "and then you'll have your own horse to ride."

Too little, too late. I looked away and blurted out, "Margie's home. She paid me for my time. I drove into town and opened up a bank account in my own name. She and Mick offered me a job on the O Bar Y for the summer, and I said I would take it."

In the time it took me to swallow, I saw the light go out of his dark hazel eyes. I recognized sadness and disbelief, regret, surprise, and a fleck of anger, but I didn't see love. I wanted to say "I'm sorry," but I couldn't.

"So what will you do now, sleep three in one bed?"

I curbed my curt response by saying, "They are going to pay me a monthly wage, plus room and board. I'll live in the little cabin next to the main house."

"And save your nickels and pennies for what? A life as a servant to someone else's desires?"

"What do you think I've been doing here? How much longer do you want me to invest in you without hope of us ever finding any solid foundation or building a lasting love?"

"What I offer you here isn't found any other place in the world. If you walk away, you'll be stuck forever in that pathetic excuse for a life, grubbing for enough money to pay taxes."

If I had not had Mick in the wings wanting me, I might never have found the courage to quit Bill, but Mick was there for me, letting me know a hundred times a day that he thought I was the best thing that had ever happened to him. I bowed my neck but didn't speak.

Bill changed his tone. He had seen Jean Senkow and her partner, Sam, in town. They had invited us up for a visit, and Bill wanted to know if I wanted to go later in the week when the back road dried up. "We'll see," I said. "What I'd like to do is get my stuff down to the O Bar Y as soon as possible."

"Then it looks like you'd better get busy and pack." He turned away.

I didn't have much to do to accomplish the task. I collected my clothes and books and tucked them into cardboard boxes. I put a few mementos from my childhood and some photographs into a suitcase. I gathered the bags that held my beading supplies, rabbit furs, and tanned hides, a cookie tin that contained strands of cobalt-blue Indian burial beads, the elk ivory belt buckle and necklace that Bill had engraved for me with images of fawns, my silver and turquoise earrings, a grouse feather fan, mink braid wraps, and deer-tail hair decorations.

Bill returned to stand in the doorway to watch me, his arms crossed over his chest. He didn't offer a single word, nor did I. If he had said he was sorry, or asked what he could do to make things better, I might have relented, but his silence acted as a goad for me to go.

He had decided to bide his time and keep his anger at bay. Was he so certain of his hold over my heart and my mind? Subtle brainwashing techniques that he had learned in the military and his intensive study of cult mentalities had proven to him that control through disparagement was the key. Make someone feel unworthy and insubstantial, convince them they are nothing and that they will never achieve anything outside of your influence, and they will stay with you forever.

What Bill didn't understand was that kindness, the precursor to all love, could break the hold of any indoctrination. Snook had been kind to me, and I had flourished. Mick and Johnny had been good to me for months, and I had blossomed. Homing in on what it felt like to be loved by others, I was determined not to turn away from that radiant beam of light.

I loaded everything I owned into the back of my station wagon. I told Kyote to stay. Looking down to the corrals, I saw Sis with her head hanging over the gate watching me. Bill was kind in the end. He followed me in the Scout down off the mountain to make sure my low-riding vehicle wouldn't high-center on the ruts or get stuck in the mud.

When we reached the O Bar Y, he offered to carry my boxes of books and clothing into the cabin, but I said I wanted to clean it first. Margie came out the door and shouted, "Hello! Come have supper. We're just sitting down for enchiladas. There's cake for dessert."

"Not tonight." Bill walked over to give her a hug. "I need to get home."

He drove away, the Scout splashing up wings of muddy water as he gunned it over the slippery road through the low-lying meadow. I followed Margie inside and sat down at the table. Mick and Johnny and Melody were arguing about something on the television. No one asked me any questions, so I didn't have to come up with any answers. After a supreme effort to take one bite of food, I swallowed over the bitter lump in my throat, and found the enchiladas to be spicy hot, the carrot cake with home-made ice cream like bites of heaven. I helped Margie clean up the dishes while Mick, the kids, and the dogs gathered in front of the television.

Later Margie said, "Do you want the couch until we can find some sheets for the cabin bed and get wood gathered for the stove out there?"

"Okay," I said. She brought me a blanket and a pillow.

The kids each hugged me and said, "Goodnight, Miss Laur."

Mick stood to the side, but he said, "We're glad you're here."

I watched Margie turn out the lights and follow him into the bedroom. I didn't feel upset or jealous. I folded my hands in prayer. "Thank you. I am full of gratitude that they have taken me in, that I have a place to stay and work to do."

I didn't sleep. I lay awake thinking of all the nights that Margie had lain in the same place on the same couch trying to come to terms with her choices and decisions. I examined my heart. I had nothing to hide and nothing to be ashamed of. If I had any talent at all, I had a talent for being honest and forthright. If anyone had asked me, I would have said that I had no ulterior motives other than to love and be loved. Mick had been the one to push for our friendship to be something more. If that upset Margie, she would have to work things out with him.

And what would happen to Bill? I had promised him during his darkest moments that I would never leave him. In the past I had gone away, sometimes for months at a time, but I had always returned. Bill was counting on that scenario based on a sacred vow, one given on my first night with him in the shifting light and shadows cast by a single candle in a land far to the north. What would happen to a girl who broke her promise?

Night Walk

Days later, Bill came by in the Scout on his way out to get the mail. He caught Margie and me coming back on horseback from an unsuccessful attempt to move the yearlings from the Point pasture to the river pasture. The cattle had spooked at the long expanse of the 165-foot wooden bridge across the Green River and refused to cross. Instead, they had crowded the wire fence along the road, collapsed it to the ground, and escaped into the boggy willow bottoms, where we had no desire to take our horses. We would have to give them a day or two to settle down and then make another attempt. Neither of us wanted to tell Mick that we had failed to execute our task, but we were laughing nevertheless, especially because of the fact that our whooping, hollering, and half-hearted cussing had done nothing to resolve the situation.

I dismounted and walked over to where Bill waited in his rig. I said hello, and he told me he was going up to see our friends Sam and Jean that evening. Did I want to go? I did. It would be lovely to see them again. I looked over at Margie. She told me to go ahead, that she would take care of dinner and the dishes. Bill said

he would pick me up on his way back. The roads out through
Schwabacher's should be passable.

After I had unsaddled and turned the horses loose, I slipped
into the main house to shower. Feeling like a teenager getting
ready for a date, I changed into clean jeans and shirt. When Bill
picked me up and noticed my nice clothes and good boots, he
warned that I would have to hop out and get all the gates. I didn't
mind. I wouldn't have to walk very far, and I could avoid the
mud holes.

We chatted like old friends on the bumpy nine-mile drive out
to the highway that would take us over to the Hoback, and then
more winding tough-to-maneuver muddy roads into Sam and
Jean's place. They had a fire going in the stove and a nice meal
nearly ready. We drank tea and shared stories. Jean showed us the
reconstruction quillwork she was doing for a museum collection.
An expert in braintanning buckskin the ancient Indian way, Bill
instructed Jean, who was just learning the art. We learned about
Sam's hunting accident; he had fallen and broken both his knees
but managed to crawl home, and then get to a doctor by using a
stick to work the brake and gas pedals on his pickup truck.

Jean and I tackled the dishes, and the guys drifted outside. I
told her that I had left Bill to go to work for the Buyers on the
O Bar Y. I confessed my great affection for Mick but said that my
decision was based on needing to earn some money. I had to find
a way to be alive in the world without so much insecurity and
worry. Jean said that sometime during the coming summer, she
would ride the twenty-something miles over to see me. I said that
I would take her up on the forest where we had been fixing fence.
The high country was coming alive with wildflowers, and I had
seen a cow elk with a newborn calf.

When we parted company it was late, and the night was dark
and cold. Bill drove with silent caution, and I didn't feel the need
to say anything, either. Things appeared peaceful between us. I
jumped out and in to get the gates, shielding my eyes from the
taillights so I could see to hook back the latches. At the fork in the

road that led up to the Flying A, Bill continued straight on. It took me a minute to realize where we were, but then I said, hearing the catch in my voice, "Bill, I need to go back to the O Bar Y."

"It's late. Why don't you come on home with me? I'll bring you back down in the morning." He kept on driving, wrenching the little rig over the rough spots as I held on with both hands.

"No. I'd better not. I have to work tomorrow. It's better if I . . . "

He slammed on the brakes, and I barely kept my head from hitting the windshield. He didn't say anything, nor did he put the vehicle in reverse. I waited a moment, thinking he was trying to figure out how to turn around, but then he said, "Well, get out."

He had no intention of taking me back to the O Bar Y. If that's where I wanted to be, then I could simply go ahead and walk. There was no sense in arguing or getting angry. That would only make matters worse. I had a rough idea where I was on the road. All I needed to do was follow it back downhill to the fork and turn left, then make my way along another four or so miles, crossing the creeks on the bridges. I would be fine. I could do this.

I picked up my purse—the one I had bought with the money Mick had given me at Christmastime. I cleared my throat and said, "Thank you for taking me to Sam and Jean's. I had a good time." When I cleared the running board and stepped out, Bill gassed the Scout and it lumbered forward, the door slamming shut of its own accord. I stayed until the headlights stopped wavering through the trees and the taillights disappeared. I waited until my eyes could adjust to the darkness and until I could try to dislodge the tight knot of fear in my throat. Maybe Bill would come back. Probably not.

It was cold, but not bitter. I had on a light coat but no gloves or scarf. My dress boots weren't warm, but walking would keep my body temperature elevated. I was fine, wasn't I? No harm done. I had dodged a bullet by not agreeing to go back up to the Flying A. The flat, no-emotion sound of Bill's "Get out" had told me that. All I needed to do was put one foot in front of the other, one step at a time, back down to the O Bar Y.

But I couldn't see. The night closed in around me with such total blackness that I couldn't see anything, not even the hand I held up in front of my face. Of course, I was in the thick trees. All I had to do was feel my way back down the road and out of the aspen grove; then I would be able to find my way. I was facing uphill next to the road. I felt with my foot until I could identify the rut, the rise, and the rut on the other side. I tried to stick with the rise. If I slipped off, the rut would still guide me. If I got out of the rut on either side, the brush and saplings would tangle against my legs in warning. I looped my purse across my shoulder to my waist and began to walk, holding out my arms like a tightrope walker in case I fell. There were no night sounds—not even any wind to stir the newly budding aspens and scattered pines.

I knew I had passed the fork in the road when I nearly stumbled into an irrigation ditch that rose up next to the rut I was walking in. A glimmer of starlight shone from its liquid surface. Like a specter, I turned back around. I could barely make out the darker outline of the forested ridge I had just descended. Then I stayed right, following the road as it curved down toward the valley.

Away from the trees, my vision increased enough for me to make a sensible guess about where to put my feet, and I picked up a bit of speed. The overcast causing the black sky had thinned, and the starlight that I saw on the ditch water now brightened the puddles in the road. I had never been so grateful for mud puddles in all my life, despite the fact that sloshing through them was destroying the boots my parents had given me for college graduation.

By the time I crossed the bridge on Little Twin Creek, I could no longer feel my toes. By the time I eased past the spooky outbuildings and cabin at Schwabacher's cow camp, my hands had gone numb. But by then I was certain I would make it. One more mile to trudge, and I would run into the big pole gate leading into the O Bar Y yard.

When I reached the door of my little cabin, I whined with relief. I pulled off my sodden, muddy, half-frozen boots and left them outside the door. I didn't bother to light a fire, but I changed

into dry long johns and a flannel shirt and crawled into the single
bed with the sagging mattress. I pulled the light-blue Hudson Bay
Four Point blanket that Bill had given me one Christmas over my
shoulders and shuddered down into what remained of my own
warmth. All the lights in the main house had been out when I
walked past; the dogs had not even barked. Mick would not know
I had come home. He would spend the night wondering about
Bill and me.

It didn't matter. What mattered is that I had stared down my
fear. I had walked alone in the night through several dark, silent
hours to find my way back to safety and sanity. I was fine. I was
learning to find my own way.

Summer Work

I immersed myself in the daily routine of helping Margie with housework, yard work, cooking, and laundry. Mimicking the accent of a young Mexican man named Juan who had worked for them the previous summer, I followed Margie around asking, "What next, Mizzus Buyer?"

"You get an A in bread making, but an F in bathroom cleaning." I followed her into the bathroom, where she pointed to the line of grime around the base of the toilet.

Juan, it seemed, had had the incredible ability to make a running leap from the barn loft, turn a complete flip, and then land on his feet in the corral below. Meanwhile, I wrenched my back trying to get the three-wheeler unstuck from a mud hole when I took hay out to feed the bulls, which were sparring in their eagerness to get out with the cows. I scuttled sideways like a hermit crab, trying not to complain.

Johnny and Melody tackled the fences around the home place, while I helped Mick tear out beaver dams. I followed him around the fields, setting head gates and building sod dams to direct the steady streams of irrigation water from Big and Little Twin Creeks. I helped him clean out his shop and the old bunkhouse. I handed him wrenches as he worked on tractors, the swather, the baler, and the stackliner, complaining about how much there was to do. And here I had thought that our winter workload of harnessing horses and feeding cattle was heavy!

"We seldom get far from a never-ending list of chores. Give me that knuckle-buster. No, the bigger one."

I had thought that all the modern conveniences like electric ovens, gas stove, refrigerator and freezer, washing machine and dryer, running water with toilets and showers, would make every-thing easier, but Mick said those things didn't decrease the need to get up early and stay up late because summers were so short. How were Margie and I getting along? Fine as far as I could tell. She never said anything about Mick, or about him and me. Was I supposed to worry about that? "Leave it be," he said.

We gathered the cattle to brand the calves. With Melody's help, Margie prepared a gigantic beef roast and all the fixings, while I helped Mick set up the corrals. He put out the necessary equip-ment for branding, earmarking, vaccinating, and doctoring. A cooler of beer along with a big bottle of whiskey appeared, along with a couple of buckets, one for disinfectant and one for the calf nuts. The O Bar Y brand had first been recorded in April 1916. Mick hadn't picked it; it had come with the ranch. Snook's grand-father, Sandy Marshall, had homesteaded across the river near the Point. When Art Mocroft bought that land, he brought the O Bar Y brand with him. In 1936 the brand transferred to Lester Mocroft, in 1940 to Richard G. Dew and Cornelia Jones Dew, and in 1963 to Earl and Joan Minyard, who then transferred it to John R. (Mick) Buyer in 1964. It sounded like a genealogy, a history written by the families who had stuck it out and those who had quit.

"Here come the hapless hordes," Mick said. "Get ready for some action."

Half a dozen pickups paraded across the bridge and up to the horse barn. Men, women, and teenagers spilled from open doors. I stood to the side amid backslapping and handshaking. No one introduced me. There was no time. The propane torches ignited. Pocketknives were sharpened. Smoke rose through the dust accompanying the bellering cries of the cows and their separated calves.

I quickly learned to wrestle the calves to the ground with a partner to hold them still so that the O, the Bar, and then the Y of the brand could be seared on quivering left hips. Then someone rushed in to take a quick slice off the end of an ear and to jab a vaccination needle under the foreleg. Another hot iron burned off the horn buds, and finally the precise cut of the bull calves' scrotums. Testicles sailed through the air and hit the "nut bucket" most every time. Dogs gobbled up the ones that missed.

For hours, the work swirled around me in a stinking, hot frenzy. Melody laughed; Johnny teased. Mick's face grew tight from the pain in his still-healing knee. Cuss words flew through the air like startled birds from dozens of dirt-caked mouths. Then we were done, the last bawling calf turned free to join the herd moving out onto fresh, now green pasture. I memorized the tally: 65 calves, 135 cows. The following day, I helped Mick drag a couple of dead bull calves to the dump behind the belching tractor, victims of infection from castration, rough handling, or a bad reaction to the vaccine. Mick swore that he was going to buy a calf table and brand every calf himself.

Johnny jokingly complained his way through weeks of fencing, and then the early haying around the house yard, barns, and corrals. He left the swather cab full of wadded tissues that he used to counter the runny nose and itchy eyes of cantankerous allergies. But at the end of June, Margie and Melody helped Johnny prepare for his trip to Michigan. He had landed a job with Fischer Brothers Aviation, an Allegheny Commuter that fed USAir in Cleveland, Columbus, and Detroit. We made a special noon dinner and his mom's chocolate cake. Bill showed up on horseback as we all stood outside to say good-bye. He didn't bother to dismount. He rode over to Johnny and presented him with a handmade pair of buckskin gloves. "Take care, flyboy," he said and wheeled his horse for home.

When my turn came to hug Johnny, I told him I would miss him, messy room and all. I asked him to please call his dad often. He assured me that he would, but first he had to find a way to get off the ranch. A stupid moose was blocking the road.

The next day, Mick and I saddled up our horses and Margie's gelding. She met us out in the yard, and we rode like the Three Musketeers to gather the pairs off the Haley meadow. The distraught mothers of the dead calves bellered and tried to run back as we moved the herd toward the forest lease for summer pasture. We encountered plenty of problems on the way: getting through gates, crossing creeks and mud-sucking sloughs, constantly pushing the small tiring calves, and turning back for bolting escapees. Any romantic notion I had of being horseback to work cattle disappeared.

Margie and Mick argued. I fell silent. The neighbors hadn't fixed their part of the fence. The beaver had felled a favorite stand of aspen trees. The general public complained about having cattle on federal land leases, but the elk had already overgrazed an upper pasture. There were badger holes everywhere. Mick's horse was getting old and infirm, and he needed another mount. By the time we finally got the cattle paired up and turned free, loneliness and regret had sickened me.

That night, I didn't go to the main house for dinner. Margie came out to my cabin to ask me what was wrong. I couldn't say. I sat there like a Raggedy Ann doll shaking my head. She went to get Mick. He sat by my side. What was it? Was I sick? I shook my head again. I wanted to go home, but I didn't know where that was. Was I unhappy?

"We never have any time together anymore except for a stolen kiss or a hug . . . " I knew we needed to be considerate of Margie and the kids. I didn't want to make waves or cause any heartbreak but . . . Who was I now? Where did I belong? I had traded in my buckskins and moccasins for jeans and boots, but if the cowgirl hat didn't fit me, why should I wear it?

Mick picked at the grease-stained cuticles on his rough hands, but he looked at me tenderly. We were going to be fine. Some afternoon when the workload eased, we would pack up a picnic and ride up on the forest. We would take salt to the cattle with the team and wagon. He would teach me how to fish.

But first he had to finish pulling the beaver dams on Mud Creek and repair the pipeline across the river so he could get water over to irrigate the Point. The fences on the Bureau of Land Management pastures still needed to be fixed. He had to weld some breaks on the flatbed trailer. Margie was waiting supper for us, so he thought we had better go do that.

When I returned to my cabin, I sat up late, writing by the light of my new kerosene lamp. I wrote a letter to my mom and dad telling them about everything we were doing on the ranch, but I kept my regrets and problems to myself. I turned down the wick and blew out the small flame. Crawling into bed, I listened to the end-of-the-evening chatter of the swallows nesting under the eaves above my head. The pair of amorous skunks had moved on after Mick had told me to put mothballs under the cabin. I watched a sliver of moon rise in the sky. I still had not made curtains for the windows. Why should I, if I didn't intend to stay? But where would I go? And why, for god's sake, was I once again sleeping alone?

Brandy

Though Mick offered to let me keep riding Poco, I wanted my own horse. I had lost my right to Sis when I left Bill, but when I hired on full-time at the O Bar Y, Mick and Margie agreed to give me $400 a month wages, room and board, plus board for a horse. After twenty-eight years of longing, I was finally in a position to be a horse owner. Eagerly I read the for-sale section in the local papers. Some traders had brought a truckload of cow ponies to the Bar Cross Ranch. Mick said, "Have Margie take you down to look them over. She's a better wheeler-dealer than me."

The next afternoon, Margie and I spent a couple hours meandering through the corrals looking at buckskins, bays, pintos, paints, Appaloosas, and sorrels. Margie found a tall, stout *grulla* that she liked. "I'll have to pay a pretty penny for him, but he should be just right for Mick. Let's call him Smoke."

When Mick unloaded the gray from the trailer, he asked, "What about you?" The expense had scared me. I couldn't choose. I worried about health, disposition, and age problems. That night, Mick called the local brand inspector, Ross Calvert, and told him

I needed a sound saddle horse. Something well broke that wouldn't buck me off. Breed and color not important.

In mid-July, Ross called back to say he had a six-year-old registered Quarter horse gelding. Bred and raised by his son. Trained up in Montana. Ross volunteered to trailer the horse out in the morning so I could "have a look-see."

Things turned into a three-ring circus on the O Bar Y. The "Marlboro men" had arrived the day before to shoot a commercial. The cameramen wanted to capture the cowboys moving cattle across the historic river bridge with the beautiful expanse of the Wind River Range in the background. Men, horses, trucks, and trailers vied for space in the front yard. Cattle milled, bellering, in the corral near the barn. A helicopter circled twice, then dropped down, landing in a cloud of dust and noise.

Ross and his wife, Darlene, arrived shortly before noon dinner. Darlene backed a bright sorrel gelding marked with four white socks and a full blaze out of the trailer. Mick and Margie's friend Darrel Winfield, a long-time Marlboro man, strolled by. He knew a little girl over in Riverton who would love to have that horse: his granddaughter. I dredged up a big wad of courage and said, "I'm trying him out today."

"You're gonna break a little girl's heart if you buy that horse," Darrel responded. He snaked a kink out of his rope and re-coiled it. As I held out my hand for the gelding to sniff, I asked Darlene his name and she said, "Brandy."

I turned my back on Darrel as he chatted with Ross and Darlene. I whispered to the horse, "This is love at first sight, Brandy, and if I can't have you, it's going to break my heart."

Brandy's registration papers showed his true name as Mighty Sublette out of Hy-N-Mighty by Hygro Leo and Sublette Susie by Sonny Sunshine. I knew nothing about bloodlines or breeding. All I cared about was whether Brandy had the kind of disposition I needed. Alert, he stood amid the noise and confusion of other horses, people, cameras, and equipment. Though a bit nervous, he didn't seem spooked. He led easily and followed me around the

yard like a dog. When Darlene boosted me up bareback, Brandy
responded to knee pressure and neck-reined with only the lead rope.

After tying Brandy in the barn, Darlene and I strolled into the
main house. Ross and Mick were drinking coffee and eating
Margie's freshly fried homemade chocolate-covered doughnuts.
Brandy was perfect, but I wanted to know why the Calverts
wanted to sell him. Ross, over six feet tall and two hundred
pounds, explained, "He's too small a horse for me, and I have
others that need riding."

Half holding my breath, I asked how much they wanted. Ross
said, "Eight hundred. Keep him the rest of the summer. Try him out.
If you like him, pay me. If you don't, I'll come and pick him up."

Everyone stared at my silence. I wasn't used to people letting
me have something of value without having to pay up front. Plus
most broke geldings were priced at $1,000 or more. I looked at
Mick. He winked at me and nodded. "Okay," I said, "it's a deal."

Mick had an ironclad rule on the O Bar Y: any new horse was
confined to the corrals for two weeks to prevent health problems
from spreading to the rest of the herd. Brandy's temporary isolation from the other horses gave us the best possible situation for
building a friendship. Each dawn before going to the main house
to fix breakfast, I hurried from my cabin to run to the barn. A
handful of alfalfa pellets in my pocket, I talked softly and walked
to Brandy as he stood forlornly in the corral's farthest corner,
looking out to where the other horses grazed on pasture. He
accepted his treats politely and haltered with ease. Then I led
him down the ranch road, walking to the river and jogging back.

With new surroundings, sights, smells, and sounds, he
spooked, shied sideways, snorted, and rolled his eyes. Soon,
though, he waited for me at the barn door, nickering a welcome.
Day by day, I took the steps necessary to build trust. I brushed his
red-gold coat, combed out his mane and tail, picked out his
hooves, taught him voice commands. Our walks turned into
rides. Though broke, young Brandy could be flighty, skittish, and

stubborn. He had as much to learn as I did. After a month, I knew that he was the horse I wanted. If I wanted to work two months without wages, Mick would pay Ross the $800. I nodded my head in agreement. The next day, Mick handed me a bill of sale for Brandy along with his registration papers.

I received a lot of ribbing over my short horse. At a little over fourteen hands, stocky-built, well-muscled Brandy was the smallest horse on the ranch. Melody called him Brand X. Margie jovially called out a line from a popular country-western song whenever I mounted up: "Shoot low, sheriff, she's riding a Shetland!" Mick took me aside and said, "Never mind. That horse will carry you to hell and back and never miss a lick." Concerned that I had never had any real schooling in horsemanship, I asked Mick to give me some pointers. Was I staying in the saddle? Was Brandy doing what I wanted him to do? When I laughed and said, "Most of the time," he nodded. "Good. You're doing just fine."

I tried a curb bit on Brandy. He hated it, chomping and tossing his head endlessly. The bit drove him nuts, and he drove me crazy. Neither of us could concentrate on anything. I tried a snaffle and a hackamore, but neither gave me the control I needed. Brandy simply fought the bit more and more, making us both a nervous wreck. Eventually I tried every bit in the tack room with similar results.

One day Mick came home and handed me a small, lightweight, low-curb bit. He had found the beat-up, rusted, bent-ringed piece of metal in the dump. In the barn loft, I sorted through old bridles and harnesses until I came up with a split-ear headstall, a chin-strap and chain, and a throatlatch. I sanded the rust off the bit, straightened the rings on the anvil, and stitched up the headstall. I added a new set of reins. Brandy never flinched when I slipped the bit in his mouth.

I used a ranch roping saddle on Brandy, but the heavy beast had too big a seat for me, and much too large a spread for his small back. I searched everywhere for a lightweight fourteen-inch seat with a high cantle and a modest horn. Melody Harding, the foreman of the Bar Cross, sold me her grandmother's well-used saddle for $120. I invested $80 to replace the worn-out stitching and get a new sheepskin and saddle strings.

Brandy's eagerness to work was a plus. Yet if we worked too long at any one task, he became sullen and unresponsive. Mick said, "You need a pair of gas feeds as an attitude adjuster." I didn't want to use spurs on Brandy because I was afraid they would hurt him, but Mick said, "Next time you go to the feed store, get a pair of inexpensive ones with short, dull rowels. All they do is poke him in the guts to make him wake up."

Brandy's short legs meant a slower than average walk and a rough-riding extended trot. Perhaps as compensation, he boasted a smooth, mile-eating jog trot, an invaluable trait for covering long distances to gather cattle. He loved to run and forever tried to push a lope into an all-out gallop. After one runaway, when I lost a rein, a stirrup, my hat, and my temper, I never gave him a chance to take the bit again.

Possessing innate cow sense, Brandy proved to be alert and good on his feet around cattle. He stayed calm in cow-packed corrals and didn't mind bringing up the drag when we moved the herd. He understood cowboy work, and he taught me day by day. Because we learned together, we turned into a good team.

Redwings

Redwings. No, not bird wings, angel wings, airplane wings, or even butterfly wings. Redwings as in shoes. Redwings became an old joke between Brandy and me. When I bought the chubby short-legged squirt, he came pre-shod with lovely trimmed feet fitted with aughts on the front and double-aughts on the back. I had seen enough horseshoeing done and tried my hand at trimming hooves often enough to know that shod feet meant back-breaking work, plus immeasurable amounts of patience and savvy. Bill had shod his horses three times each summer, producing liberal amounts of sweat and a tangible blue streak of cuss words that altered the sky.

Snook had had more patience. He allowed me the use of a pair of nippers and a rasp to work on his old palomino gelding, Nugget, who politely held up his feet for me and never jerked back or kicked. And I had once watched Snook and Bill tussle with a fancy-pants snorting mare until she ended up roped, thrown, and tied down before they could work on her feet. If I planned on being a real cowgirl, I had to shoe my horse. I used some of my carefully hoarded money to buy the basic tools: nippers, a rasp, a hoof pick and knife, a shoeing hammer, a box of nails, and two sets of shoes.

By August, Brandy had lost one hind shoe and the other shoes needed replacing. Mick helped me pull the old loose shoes one day, but then he got busy repairing equipment, and I didn't want to bother him again. Old Tom Astle, a retired government trapper who had come up to help with haying, offered advice when he stopped by to check on me. "I'd do the job for you myself if I were still able," he said around his hand-rolled cigarette. "Hell of a tough go, but you'll get it." He moseyed away to gas up the baler tractor.

Gentle and calm in the corral, Brandy could care less if I was shoeing or snoozing. His major fault lay in the fact that he was a consummate leaner. This meant that in order to work on his feet, I had to stand doubled over like a circus contortionist with my nose nearly on the ground and my ample rump stuck up in the air. Unladylike, to say the least, even if no one saw me.

I read books. I read articles in *Western Horseman*. I asked questions of old-timers. I wrote long, detailed letters to my dad's friend Oscar Lindholm, who had once shod horses for the Army cavalry. A staunch defender of doing things nature's way, Oscar fitted the shoe to the shape and size of the horse's hoof. Slapping on a shoe, then rasping the hoof to fit the shoe was considered a cardinal sin. I tried to follow the correct procedure. I told Brandy that horseshoeing was not brain surgery. It was a necessary skill that I could learn. But after many attempts, I admitted defeat. My willing mind opposed the protest of my aching back, jellied legs, and numb hands. When I complained to Mick, he said, "Call Melody Harding. She's tough as nails. She shoes all her own horses."

Margie and Melody Harding were good friends. Plus she and Mick's Melody were barrel-racing buddies. They kept their names straight by calling Melody Buyer "Melo" and Melody Harding "Medley." When I hesitated to make the phone call, Mick said, "She is strictly a no-bellyaching, do-the-job-right kind of gal. She can pick up an anvil, carry it across the corral, and not even break a sweat. Don't worry about it. Just call her and ask. If she can't do it, she'll say she can't do it."

On the appointed day, I caught Brandy and whispered in his ear as he ate his treats: today you're going to get a new pair of redwings. His ears went up, his eyes grew wide, his nostrils flared, his belly swelled with a giant breath. Then he deflated himself with a huge, resigned sigh, something like a kid going to the dentist or a husband having to accompany his entertainment-starved wife to a movie. Then he stood sleepily in the barn tied to a manger until Melody arrived.

I immediately admired many things about Melody, not the least of which was that she could carry on a good old gossipy conversation with her mouth full of horseshoeing nails. Petite, buxom, athletic, and beautiful, Melody kept her long blond hair tucked up under her cowboy hat as she swung the heavy hammer to shape Brandy's shoes. He must have liked her from the get-go because whenever she tapped on his hoof, he politely raised that one leg and rebalanced his weight on the other three. He didn't lean on her or act impatient or ill at ease. He maintained his status as a perfect gentleman for more than an hour. Melody thought him a "sweetheart."

I figured that he sensed my lack of confidence so he took advantage of my ineptness. "Just like a kid, eh?" she said as she patted him on the neck. "Let's trim the overgrown hair between his forelock and mane and around his ears," she said to me. "You want to look handsome, don't you, son?" Brandy looked at her out of the corner of his eye, but he also nodded his head as if she had cued his consent.

When I hinted that Brandy didn't like anyone messing with his ears, Melody didn't ignore me; she simply chose not to believe that the pint-size horse would give her any trouble. She pulled a pair of clippers from her saddlebags and plugged them in. Nothing I could have said would have prepared her for Brandy's reaction when she clicked on the switch. He not only tried to go over backward to get away from the buzzing clippers, he also stepped squarely on her foot. She quickly moved back and turned off the clippers.

"Guess he doesn't like the sound of these." She tried again. Another burst of crashing 1,000-pound horse against the stall wall. "Okay, we'll get a blindfold."

I wanted to suggest that we simply trim Brandy's mane with a scissors as I normally did, but I didn't feel qualified to interfere. Plus, I was curious. Did Melody know some horse-dealing techniques that might help me understand how to work with Brandy in a better way?

She picked up a sweater that she had shed before starting to shoe and approached Brandy with a calm hand. He wasn't keen on allowing her to tuck the sweater under the straps of his halter so that the material covered his eyes, but he didn't put up a fuss. He quivered all over and snorted, but he waited until the clippers buzzed before he blew up again. With gentle persistence, Melody tried several more times to accomplish the task at hand. Brandy, for his part, decided that she was not going to succeed.

"Well, I don't want to whomp him like he was one of my own horses. Any suggestions?" she asked. I told her I just used a pair of scissors and hacked away the best I could. She slipped off Brandy's blindfold, to which he responded by dropping his head and sighing as if to say, "Thank god that is over. Do I have to endure anything else?"

While Melody snipped, I brushed. She combed out his mane, and I worked on his tail. When we were finished, and I led him outside in the sunshine to turn him loose in the pasture with his pals, she said, "He's beautiful. Ever think of showing him? I think you told me he's registered."

"No, I just want him to be a cow horse." What I didn't say is that I didn't have a truck or a trailer with which to haul a horse, and even if I had, I wasn't cowgirl enough to load up Brandy and drive around the county to different shows. I didn't want to be out in the world at large or deal with anything like competitive events.

"Well, if you ever change your mind, let me know. I'll give you some pointers. He'd be very good in halter class or in western pleasure."

I invited her in for a glass of tea. "Margie make a fuss about you and Mick?" she asked as we walked up to the house. I said, "Not really" and asked her how she knew about Mick and me. She laughed and said, "Everyone knows. The gossipmongers have been having a free-for-all." She told me not to worry about it. She was glad because at least now they weren't talking about her. "Do you think that horses and women have a lot in common?" I asked. I had learned a lot during my years with Bill, but I felt like I was constantly looking over my shoulder in fear of a reprimand. Now I was learning a lot from Mick, but I felt more relaxed and eager to do my work. I didn't feel afraid. I sensed that the hardness I had developed with Bill was softening because Mick was easier on me.

"Well," Melody said, "a horse will follow you anywhere if you give it enough kind words and occasional praise. I suppose most women are the same way."

Hard Work Never Hurt Anyone

Breakfast was over by daybreak. While Margie tended to house chores, Mick took care of maintaining the equipment, and I helped whichever one of them needed me the most. By the time the sun had risen high enough to evaporate the heavy dew that gathered every night at that cool elevation, Mick would have a new patch of hay marked out with the swather. Melo took over to complete the cutting. If an earlier-cut field had dried enough to bale, Margie headed out on the baler. Mick turned to fighting the beaver to keep the water off the meadows or wrestled the big stackliner across the ditches to pick up the gradually accumulating bales stretched out over acres along the river. Some days, Old Tom Astle drove out from town to help us. I went wherever I was told to go to learn the routine. The pressure was on because there were only so many days left until the fall's first snows.

Mick insisted that I go with him one day so he could teach me how to swath hay.

I studied the huge machine with all its gears and levers and the slicing, rotating header and told him that I would stay in and get noon dinner ready, that I would do the laundry.

I didn't want to help with the haying if it meant I had to drive equipment. I knew nothing about machinery. Engines terrified me. I would gladly turn bales in the field or stack bales by hand, but that was it. Mick took off his hat and swiped at the sweat on his brow. "Listen, sassy pants. Does that horse of yours eat hay?"

I turned to face him. He said, "Here's the deal. I need every hand I can get, and you've got two of them." He told me that I was smart and competent, and that it was not as hard as I thought. I cussed as I ran to the house to tell Margie where I would be, then dashed back out and climbed up into the cab of the growling swather.

Mick put the monster machine in gear, and we trundled off to the Haley meadow. I scrambled on and off to open the gates. "See," Mick said, "you're already more help than you know."

He walked me through the steps one at a time as he engaged the sickle bars and lowered the header into a stand of thigh-high waving timothy grass. Then he increased the sickle speed and inched the machine forward, showing me the rabbit and turtle symbols on the lever: rabbit goes faster; turtle goes slower. "Got that?"

I nodded.

"The cut hay is combed into the middle of the path, where the teeth pick it up and feed it through rollers. That crushes the stems to help the grass dry. The hay's left in a swath behind the machine. That's why they call it a swather."

I hollered to be heard over the noise. "How is it different from a mower?"

"A mower leaves the hay scattered flat in the field, and then it has to be raked before baling. The swather's more expensive, but it saves time and money in the long run."

"Who taught you?"

"The Three Stooges: me, myself and I." Mick explained that I needed to watch the irrigation ditch on my left. From that high up, I could see the boundary it created around the field. He told me to follow the ditch, to never turn sharp, turn smooth, to watch out for birds' nests or fawns hidden in the grass. I wouldn't always be able to avoid them, but I should try. When in doubt, stop.

Mick made several rounds of the meadow. He stopped the swather and squirmed out of the seat, told me to try, and pulled me into place. My short legs didn't reach the floor, and it was a stretch to get to the steering, so we adjusted everything to fit my stature. He laughed. "You look like a little chipmunk trying to drive this thing. But you can do it. Melo does just fine."

He coached me through the initial steps, and then I reached for the throttle—only I wasn't looking at the rabbit or the turtle or which one was going which way. I looked straight ahead, down into the eye-blurring action of the sickles and the spinning of the head. I searched for any innocent animals in the path of the machine. I moved the throttle, and the swather shot forward, the sickles gouging up huge chunks of sod that crashed through the rollers.

"Jesus Christ! Don't take Mother Earth with you!" Mick yelled. He put his hand over mine and eased back on the power.

The underlying anger startled me. I had only heard that tone once before, when I had tried to push on the rear end of the pickup that he had mired in a swale crossing. "Quit!" he had scolded. "That'll do about as much good as a piss-ant pushing on the Empire State Building. I'll have to walk back and get a tractor to pull us out. You stay here and tear out that goddamned beaver dam that made this bog hole."

This time he said, "You're okay." He put his hand on my shoulder. "Just a rough start. Try again."

"I don't want to. I don't want to be here. I want to go back up on Tosi Creek with Snook, where he cuts his hay with horses."

"If you were up there, you'd be dealing with a pack of idiotic dudes trying to teach them how to fly-fish."

"That would be better than being stuck inside this hot cab surrounded by diesel fumes and noise!" I swallowed back the bile that rose into my throat.

"Listen, Gallantry, you can't quit me now. I need you here. You can do this. Just settle down."

"I can't settle down. I feel like a fly trapped in a glass jar."

"Go on. Try again."

I pulled forward, inching the machine against the tall grass. Halfway around the field, I stuck it in the ditch. "Not a problem. Scoot over." Mick squished in next to me. With a great deal of moaning and creaking on the part of the machine, he eased it back on track. "Go again." He moved to stand behind me once more.

I gained a bit of courage and shoved the throttle a bit at a time toward the rabbit symbol. I looked in the rearview mirror. Rows of fluffed hay spilled out behind us. I glanced back to see a young sandhill crane running. Before I could react, the spinning header grabbed it.

"Don't stop," Mick warned. He put his hand over mine on the throttle. "Keep going. Nothing you can do about it now."

"But it's—"

"Dead. It happens. We're not stopping until we finish this field. Goose it up a little more."

I got hot and tired and thirsty. My right shoulder ached, and my right hand went numb. My head pounded until I thought that my eyes would pop right out. Finally, at dusk, Mick shut down the swather. We left it standing in the unfinished field like a monolith in honor of the setting sun. We walked back to the ranch, this time hand in hand because there was no one to see us. When he said, "See there. No lives lost," I didn't mention the flattened, mangled crane.

Margie had a pot roast with potatoes and carrots waiting on the table. When she asked how everything had gone, Mick said not bad, but he hinted that perhaps I could be trained on the baler. The idea of spending all day on a creeping tractor dragging a clunking, dust-spewing baler didn't appeal to me, but I voiced no opinion. I ate my supper, did the dishes so Margie could do bookwork, took a quick shower, and went back to my cabin. My back ached. My legs hurt. My abdomen felt swollen and hot. My period had come early. Well, I told the log walls, at least that's better than it being late! I confessed to the woodstove that I had taken to stealing Jim Beam from the kitchen cupboard when no one was looking to deal with pain. I lay on my bed in the stuffy cabin, wishing I had a fan or that I could open the windows or the door to let in some air, but a door and windows without screens let in hordes of annoying, blood-sucking mosquitoes. Who could I talk to?

At breakfast the next morning, I asked Mick for the day off. I told him I had to go to a doctor. Would he please go with me, would he drive me into town? The panic in his eyes made him look as if I had asked him to murder his mother. "Why do you need to see the sawbones?"

Exhaustion. Horrible periods. Birth control.

He ducked his head in apology. He couldn't get away. He had too much to do.

Sawbones

Filling out forms at the clinic wasn't easy. I had no medical history, but I seemed to have every ailment present on the long list of complaints. When had I had my last period: a week ago. Had I ever been pregnant: not sure. I had an uneasy feeling that the long spells of vaginal bleeding I had suffered during my years with Bill might have been early-onset miscarriages. When had I had my last pelvic exam: nine or so years ago. That gave me pause. Had that many years passed since my mother had taken me to a gynecologist for the first time?

The nurse stuck my finger and had me pee in a cup. She took my blood pressure, sighed, and then took it again. She fiddled with the scale, perhaps, like me, in hopes that it would register a few less pounds. She told me to undress and settled me on the icy exam table with my legs up in the air suspended in stirrups, and then the doctor came in to wrench me open and take a tissue sample. I kept my eyes squeezed shut and listened to the two of them whisper.

Dressed again, I sat on a stool. Doc Johnston came in, studied my one-page chart, and then eyed me over the top of his glasses.

Was I "the one up at the Buyer place"? I cleared my throat and said yes. "How is Mickey's knee?" I said it still hurt Mick a lot, but that he was getting around okay. "Good. Those surgeons over in Jackson Hole know what they're doing. They patch up a lot of skiers. I figured they'd do a decent job on an old cowpoke."

He looked at all the boxes I had checked. "You're here because . . . "

"Mostly because of fatigue, and I have bad periods."

"Pretty common for a woman your age. Lots of solutions for that. How bad?"

I didn't know what he meant. Should I tell him how much Jim Beam it took to make the pain go away? Or that I rolled around on the floor trying to get the aching to ease? He asked me how many tampons I used each day, and how long my period lasted.

Nine or ten super ones on the worst days, and usually seven to eight days.

He took off his glasses, sat up straighter in his chair, and asked why I hadn't had a checkup in nine years. Because I had lived pretty remote and had no money.

He nodded. "Sexually active."

Was he making a statement or asking a question? I whispered, "Yes."

"Birth control?" He scribbled on the paper.

"Rhythm method." That got his attention.

"When I was younger, I kept a calendar . . . but now . . . I mean . . . he uses condoms."

I had never said that word out loud before. It had been hard enough for me to buy a package of rubbers at the grocery store when I had ridden into town with Johnny earlier in the spring. Doc Johnston wanted to put me on birth control pills to slow down the bleeding. I was very anemic and had a slight bladder infection, and my blood pressure was too high. He wanted to draw more blood to check my cholesterol level and thyroid. "I'd guess," he said, "and I'm a pretty good guesser, that you're also working too hard. Lifting heavy stuff? Like bales and calves and saddles and salt blocks?"

"I need this job, and I—"

Doc Johnston held up his hand. "You've got to take better care of yourself. Ease off. Pace yourself. Eat more red meat. Mickey's got enough cows on that place to give you a steak now and then. He's a pretty lucky man to have you in his pocket."

I blushed, and Doc Johnston smiled at me. "And I'm glad he's got you, too. I didn't much like the idea of him being up there alone."

He handed me a prescription and gave me directions to the drug store. He told me to call him if I had any problems, and to tell Margie to get in to see him. She was overdue for her checkup. Before I left, he raised his finger at me for emphasis. He had had a long-time patient and friend who stopped having her annual exams because she figured she was too old. She was going through menopause, but she met a new man, and they had stopped out somewhere in the sagebrush to make love. She thought it odd when she began to bleed and the bleeding didn't quit. She finally came in to see the doctor. But it wasn't her period returning; it was cancer. She was dead within a matter of months. He said, "You tell Margie that. Tell her to get in here pronto."

I didn't get to tell Margie anything. When I returned to the ranch, she and Mick were engaged in a full-fledged argument about my being gone for the day. "You can't keep this girl locked up here on the ranch working all the time," Margie said. "She'll go stir-crazy like I did. We'll get the blankety-blank hay in eventually."

Mick shoved back his chair and grabbed his hat. "I'll be in the shop!"

Margie backed away. "I hate it when he yells at me."

"Margie, that's not yelling. That's being emphatic or frustrated. You haven't ever seen a bad temper. You never heard Bill when he was mad."

"The son-of-a-pooch! I'm going out to bale what I didn't finish yesterday."

Needing to talk to somebody, I called Melody Harding and lucked out to catch her in the house in the middle of the day. She told me that I was probably not talking to the right woman. When

she had been shipping cattle the previous fall, she got her period
way out in the middle of nowhere. She soaked through her jeans
as well as the saddle. The guys took a break for lunch, but she
refused to get off her horse. There was no way she was going to
give the idiots a chance to tease her. She told them she would stay
mounted and keep an eye on things in case they had any cow
trouble. And she stayed in the saddle all afternoon and into the
evening. She never got off once, not even to pee. It was dark by
the time she loaded the horses into trailers to come home. She sat
on her slicker in the truck cab to drive back to the Bar Cross,
thinking that her bladder was going to burst.

Margie did go to see Doc Johnston. She was worrying about
her hair falling out, that it came out by the handful when she
brushed it, and she found many loose strands on her pillow each
morning. Doc Johnston told her it was due to stress, not age.
When she asked him what to do, he told her to get out of the
stressful situation. He quizzed her like a kindly father, though he
already knew, like everyone else in the Kendall Valley, that Mick
had two women on his ranch, one his wife and the other his . . .
what to call me? Girlfriend? Lover? Mistress? None of those
seemed to fit. When I said "hired hand," people looked at me with
a small smile, as if to say, "Hired for what?" Margie, however, with
her beautiful sense of humor, called me her "wife-in-law."

The tight-knit community of ranch wives in the valley may
have wanted to stand in judgment of me, but Margie championed
me, embraced me as her friend, and gave them no excuse not to
like me despite our somewhat unusual circumstances. They all
knew the story of Mick and Margie's life, or at least the parts of it
garnered from gossip and guessing. Margie bragged on me and
explained that I had been an indentured servant to a mountain
man. She and Mick had rescued me. They had picked me up like a
stray pup wandering the highway and given me a home. Margie
made fun of the situation, but she never made fun of me. Somehow, we worked it out. If there was any jealousy on her part, she
chose not to show it. If there was insecurity on my part, I tried

not to reveal that. Both of us focused on putting the ranch first, because without the ranch, none of us would have a home. We put Mick second because without him, running the ranch would be nearly impossible.

Baler Time

Before heading out to cut the Mud Creek field, Mick said, "Your mountain man called. He ordered me to tell you to come and get your goats." Excited, I asked if I could have them. Mick said no. He would not run goats. They stank. They would eat all of Margie's flowers and trees. That would mean "hell to pay." They would climb on the vehicles and equipment. I argued. They didn't stink. I would build a pen and take care of them. I promised Mick that he wouldn't have to do a thing except enjoy the fresh milk, butter, cheese, and ice cream. The mention of homemade ice cream did the trick. He agreed to help me build a stout pen with the hog wire out behind the shop.

A few days later, as I gassed up the cab-less Massey Ferguson tractor, I flagged Bill down as he drove through the yard in his Scout. I jogged up to the window and said, breathless, that I would come and get the goats. He told me not to bother. That he had sold them. Pain and sadness rifled through me. I dropped my head to stare at the toe of my boot.

"Is this what you're doing now?" Bill said. "Running a baler?"

"I've gotten good at greasing the zerks and changing the spools of baling twine."

Mick came out of the shop and asked what was going on. Bill said that he wanted to let Mick know that he was taking off into the hills with a saddle horse and packhorse. There wouldn't be anyone up at the Flying A for a couple weeks.

"Good enough," Mick said.

"Have fun." Bill pointed the remark at me and drove off.

The fact remained that the tractor had to crawl across the earth slowly in order to tow the noisy beast that gobbled up the swaths of hay and packed them into tight, fragrant bales. I liked being out in the open air no matter how hot it got on the days when I dumped water on my head to stay awake and took sleepy-eyed breaks in the shade of the tall tractor wheels. Coyotes and deer and the majestic cranes kept me company. Herons floated up from the river, beaver paddled in the creeks, moose hid in the willows, red-winged blackbirds called from the reed-choked sloughs. I daydreamed as hawks drifted in circles above my head, always eyeing the opportunity to dive on an unsuspecting rodent flushed into the open.

My biggest complaint about running the baler was the permanent crick I developed in my neck from looking back over my shoulder to make certain the drying swaths fed into the chute with the right timing. Too fast, and the baler jammed. Too slow, and it took forever to make one round of a field. In some spots the hay lay thick, and in others thin, which meant that I needed to be constantly vigilant, changing gears from first to third depending on the conditions. I also developed the malady that Mick called "rump-sprung" and that Margie referred to as "sitting on two golf balls." My butt bones never ceased hurting even when I lay in bed at night.

I sometimes stopped the tractor but left the baler running with its persistent thunk, thunk, thunk as I hopped off to do a series of jumping jacks or run in place. I never got off the back of the tractor near the power take-off after Mick scolded me severely: "I

knew a guy whose pants leg got caught in the spinning gear. It
mangled his leg so badly that he had to have it amputated. You
stay away from the back of the tractor."

If I broke down in the hayfield, which happened more often
than not, then I had a long walk in to the ranch to find Mick to
help me. Sometimes the knotters stopped tying the twine, or the
shear pin broke, or the tractor quit for no good reason and refused
to restart. One time the whole chain assembly flew off through
the air like a broken rubber band. I searched for an hour before
finding it in the field twenty-five yards away. That shut us down
for days.

But Mick always knew what to do. Though he cussed and
fussed about wasting time, he knew how to fix things, even if he
had to root through the dump for parts. The mechanical and
welding skills that he had learned as a teenager from his Uncle
Art served him well. When he couldn't find or make what he
needed, he sent Margie into Big Piney to the parts store. Sometimes, wearying of the lonely routine on the ranch, she left to
visit friends, look at replacement bulls, or talk to the people at
the agricultural extension office.

When I wasn't on the baler, I helped Mick grease the other
equipment or walked the extensive hayfields, turning bales on
their sides so that Mick could pick them up more easily with the
stackliner. He, on the other hand, had mastered the art of driving
the three-wheeler around the meadows so that he could use his
good leg to shove the bales that had landed flat out of the baler
over onto their sides. The haystacks grew into long, flat-topped
structures that looked like man-made golden mesas. On rainy
days, Mick and I spent our time fixing the stack yard fences to
keep out the moose and elk.

One evening, Mick roared out on Johnny's motorcycle to bring
me a hamburger wrapped in foil. "Margie sent your supper," he
yelled over the roar of both machines. "Some of your friends
stopped by. I told them you were out in the hayfield and couldn't
be bothered."

I choked on my first hurried bite. "What?" He repeated himself.

"Who were they?" I didn't have many friends in the area.

"Hell, I don't know. I sent them away."

I gobbled down the burger, crushed the foil in my pocket, climbed back on the tractor, put it in gear, and trundled off into the setting sun. I strung together a bunch of muffled cuss words that were not as nice as "son-of-a-pooch." I had been on the baler for nine hours without a break, and Mick had sent my friends—whoever they were—away. Okay. Fine. I would perch on my raw butt with my neck cricked and keep going until the tractor ran out of gas, until the Buyer family recognized that I was a worthy hand.

Driving around in circles, hauling the baler beast, gave me an excruciating amount of time to examine my heart. I did think about Bill, more than I cared to admit. I wondered how he was but doubted that he was happy. I knew that in his odd, awkward way he had loved me and cared about me; that he had never meant to hurt me—nor I him. Hadn't we both had the dream of being wonderful to one another? But I would never know, even if I tried to convince myself otherwise, what was wrong with me, what I had lacked, why he couldn't love me the way I needed to be loved. So I had died a little every day knowing that he didn't love me the same way I loved him. Now I feared the same situation was happening with Mick: wanting him so much, loving him so much, and knowing that as much as he might want to, he wasn't able to love me back. Is that what had happened to Margie? The withering away, the drying up inside, the knowing that no matter what we did to prevent the attrition of our goodness, we ended up becoming bitter and resentful, angry, harping old women.

Breakdown

I walked into the main house to find Mick pacing the living room and Margie sobbing at the table, the top of her hair curled up in pink rollers and mascara running down her cheeks.

"What?" I said. "Did something happen?"

"You talk to her," Mick said. "I don't know what to do with her."

"No, you talk to him. He's the one that makes everything so difficult."

"Okay, first, is everyone all right? Are the kids fine? No one died?"

Margie shook her head and kept crying. Mick walked over to a straight-backed chair under the window and plopped down.

"Well, I can't help with anything if no one is going to say anything. Margie?"

She couldn't answer. Mick looked down at his boots, which hadn't been saddle-soaped or polished in a month of Sundays.

What should I do? Walk out and leave them to work it out, whatever it was? But if it was about me, and it probably was, then I needed to stay.

"Mick," I said. "Come over here."

He gave me a sideways glance like I was a schoolteacher telling him to get up in front of the class and apologize for something, but he rose and took a chair at the head of the table. Margie was sitting directly across from him, and I was in the middle.

"Somebody start. Say something. If it's about me, that's fine. Do you want me to leave?"

"No," Mick said with such force that Margie picked her head up off her arms. "I can't run this place without some help. I need you here. I want you here."

"Margie, come on. Say whatever you have to say. We're here to listen. Maybe we can work something out."

She choked on her words: "I'm old and ugly--and you're young and pretty. And I'm fat—and you're not."

"That's a laugh." I reached over to touch her arm. We had both been trying to lose weight, so we had started a competition to see who could be the first to lose ten pounds. "You are way ahead of me on that score. And you're not old or ugly, either."

"Yes, I am. Nobody wants me. Mick has you, and you have him, and I don't have anyone."

"Margie . . . " I couldn't think of anything else to say.

"Mick, say something," I commanded gently, but he only shook his head and looked at his hands. He had taken off his black cowboy hat, and his receding hairline sparkled with sweat.

"What I want to know"—Margie sniffled and blew her nose and put the tissue on the mounting pile next to her on the table— "is if you love each other."

I hesitated, waiting for Mick to say something first, but he didn't even look up.

"My dad taught me that honesty is always the best policy." I sat straighter and folded my hands in front of me. I swallowed and said, "Yes, I love Mick. I have for some time."

Panic set in, and my palms turned damp. My heart flitted around like a caged canary. What if Mick didn't say anything to acknowledge me?

Margie nodded her head. She stopped crying. We both looked
at Mick. We would not stop staring at him until he said something.
The room was so quiet, I could hear the creek running below the
house. Nearby, a raven squawked out a single cry that sounded
like a heart breaking.

"Yes." He shoved back his chair. "Yes, I love Laurie. I love her
because she's here for me—she's here for me, and I need the help."
He sounded angry, as if he didn't want to love me but couldn't
help it.

"I'm here for you, too," Margie said.

"No, you're not, goddamn it! You're off gallivanting around the
country or down in Arizona."

"I'm here right this minute cleaning this house and cooking
your meals and working in the hayfield every blasted day. I—"

"Oh, to hell with this!" Mick grabbed his hat and stalked out.
"I'll be in the shop," he offered as he slammed the door.

Margie started to cry again.

"Tell me what to do," I said.

"I don't know. I don't know. It's always this way. His way. Never
my way. I just want someone to love me for who I am."

"Do you think I should leave? Margie, would it help if I moved
away, got a job in town?"

"No. You'd better stay. He wants you, not me. I'm all used up.
Anyway, I'll be gone in the fall. It's the stupidest thing, but I feel
less guilty if you're here with him."

We moved around the kitchen like robots, getting pork chops
and corn on the cob ready for dinner. Margie said that she had
come home that summer reserving judgment on everything until
she could get a feel for what was going on with Mick and me.
Was it just a fling? Something we would both get over? She
reminded me that I was pretty young. Didn't I want my own
home and children someday? She wondered whether she and
Mick had any love left for each other. They had never talked
about divorce. Not really. Not except in anger. I reminded her of
her comment to me that day coming back from Idaho Falls about

wanting a divorce. Is that what she really wanted after they had
stayed together this long?

"We stuck it out for the kids, but now they're grown and getting
lives of their own. I keep hoping that Mickey will sell out and join
me in Arizona."

"You're sleeping in the bedroom again. Isn't that a good sign?"

"A lot of good that's done," Margie said. "He keeps to his own
side of the bed as if I have the plague."

She buried her head in the books at her desk as I stirred a
pan of bubbling vanilla pudding that I had just taken off the
stove. The front door slammed open as Mick burst into the house.
"I need help!"

Margie and I stumbled over each other to get there. He was
limping badly, and his face was flour-paste white.

Margie ordered him to sit down and asked him what happened.
I grabbed his arm and helped him get over to the table. He lowered
himself into a chair. I took his hat off and put it on his recliner.
Was it his knee?

"No. Dropped a goddamned heavy part on my foot. Get my
boot off before it swells too much."

I wrestled with Mick's too-tight boot as he gritted his teeth
and groaned. The phone rang, and Margie answered. I looked up
to see her talking as she stretched the phone cord over the kitchen
counter. I gingerly pulled Mick's sock off. He could rotate his ankle,
but his big toe looked like a blackened tomato, and the top of his
foot was turning the color of eggplant.

"Goddamn it," he said, "I've got work to do."

Margie put her hand over the mouthpiece on the phone and
said, "It's Melody Harding. She wants us to—"

"No! Absolutely not. You go," Mick pointed at Margie, "if you
want to, if you have to. But Laurie is not going. I need her here!"

"We can't go," I heard Margie say. "We need to take Mick to
the doctor."

I didn't take Mick to the doctor that afternoon, Margie did. He
told me later that Doc Johnston had heated the tip of a paperclip

with a match and then burned a hole through his mashed toenail. The hematoma had sprayed blood forth with the force of a little geyser.

"What did Doc Johnston say?" I asked.

"He told me I'd live. That it was a long way from my heart."

Convert

I discovered shelves of romance novels in the cookhouse, right alongside the Louis L'Amour Westerns that Johnny liked. Whenever I had the smallest slice of free time, I buried my nose in the sensual trials and tribulations of imaginary characters. The stories always turned out the same, with the rogue guy winning the heart of the beautiful girl, but I became addicted to the fictional way in which they worked out their problems.

Whenever Mick caught me in the act, he would tease, "What are you doing? Reading smut?"

"It takes my mind off things. Don't you ever read?"

"I read the stock papers. I don't have time to read books. The only one I ever read was in grade school. Some story about a boy and his dog."

"You never read another book?"

"Never had to. Just followed Pop and Dad down the cow path. Besides, the only things I'm interested in are current events and politics, the things that affect the viability of the ranch."

That stuff was boring to me, but Mick advised me to pay attention to the governmental decisions that were keeping family ranching alive. He suggested strongly that I start reading the stock papers, and the local paper, too. Maybe then, he hinted, I would understand what we were going through. Who did he mean by "we"? All of our neighbors, which was a comparative term. He told me to think about the fact that he was the only working-class man on that section of the Green River. Lowell Hansen at the Flying A owned Jackrabbit Bus Lines. The Carney family, flanking the O Bar Y on one side, owned Superior Graphite, and flanking us on the other was Jack Schwabacher from the Levi-Strauss family. The Bar E Bar, the Black Butte, and the Quarter Circle 5 were working ranches, but they were run by foremen, not by the absentee landowners, who came only during hunting season or for part of the summer.

I confessed that I had not known the situation. Mick explained that the Carneys and Jack Schwabacher lived most of the time in other states. They had other businesses. They were not dependent on ranch income for their livelihoods. In fact, they used the losses on their ranches as tax write-offs.

Others, like the Tylers, Alexanders, and Papes, were multigenerational families working ranches in Sublette County, and every last one of them was struggling to make ends meet, like Mick and Margie. If they were not battling the weather, low cattle prices, high feed prices, and exorbitant interest rates to buy equipment or take out an operating loan for another year, they were struggling to put kids through college, pay health-care costs, get reliable hired help, or keep their marriages together.

Mick picked up the *Pinedale Roundup.* He wanted me to listen to an opinion column written by the editor, Ric Samulski. It was titled "Thank you, David Stockman." I felt stupid, but I didn't know who David Stockman was. Mick said, "President Reagan's budget director. Samulski says that Stockman came down strongly against more handouts for the farmers and doesn't understand

why the taxpayers of the United States should be asked to come to
the financial rescue of those farmers in trouble."

Mick read the long piece out loud, set down the paper, and
lowered his reading glasses to look at me.

"That irks me," I said. "Especially his comparison of the family
farm to hula-hoop manufacturers. What kind of thinking is that?"

"You tell me. Sounds to me like the whole world is going to hell
in a hand basket."

"We can't just let him say things like that . . . It's our way of life.
Do you think Margie would mind if I used her desk?"

Mick told me to "have at it," so I dusted off the electric typewriter and wrote a title to my editorial response: "Where would
you be, Ric?" When I had finished outlining all the reasons why
people needed to support family farms and ranches, I finished
my composition by saying, "Where will America's heart and her
hope be when the family farm is gone and the land is owned by
nameless, faceless and gutless corporations? I think all of us need
crying towels . . . the time will come for mourning." I signed the
letter "Respectfully, Laurie Wagner." Feeling like a crusader with a
cross, I carried it into the living room to read it to Mick. I wanted
to know what he thought.

He offered an affirmative shake of his head. If people in the
Green River Valley had not heard about me before, they would
know me now. Did that mean he would mind if I sent the letter
in to the paper? He said, "It's no skin off my back" and even
offered to give me a stamp and run it out to the mailbox for me.
Yes, I sounded young and idealistic, but when people criticized
those who farmed, ranched, logged, mined, or worked the land,
it fired me up.

"Just don't go getting too environmentalist on me," Mick said.
"We don't need tree huggers, either."

But did Mick think I was right? If others wanted to criticize,
shouldn't they first have to experience the lifestyle they were
condemning? Why didn't they go out and spend some time

harvesting a crop that had been damaged by hail, or go through a
brutal calving season, or work with a chain saw for twelve hours a
day, or go underground into the darkness to dig out the fuel that
heated their homes, or get their hands dirty working in the oil
and gas fields for the fuel that powered their cars and trucks?

"You're catching on. There's a lot more to what we're doing
every day than just paying the bills."

One day when he was rustling through a box of papers looking
for a deed, Mick said, "Here, look at this." He handed me his
Army discharge papers. The document showed his occupation as
"cowpuncher." How funny, I said. Like saying "cowpoke." Why did
they use that word?

"That's what they were called back then."

"Why not 'cowboy'?"

"I'm not a cowboy. Don't call me a cowboy."

When I asked why not, he said that "cowboy" was reserved for
rodeo bums or bronc busters, or the guys on horseback who took
care of cattle out on the range, or the ones who doctored cattle
horseback in feedlots.

Should I call him a rancher? He thought that was better, but
someone could own a ranch and not have anything to do with
cattle. "Some dopes are even raising llamas and emus."

I wanted to know what to call him. "Cowman, I guess. Bred,
born, and raised by men who ran one of the earliest strains of
Hereford cattle found in the West."

"Are you a Hereford man, too?"

"Always was. For most of my life. Then old Ross sold me the
black ballys. First black cattle I ever owned. I had to apologize to
Dad when I bought them—even though he was dead. Didn't want
him turning over in his grave."

Was he glad that he had switched to the crossbred cows? Their
calving performance impressed him. They were raising good,
stout calves. He liked it that they didn't get pinkeye, cancer eye, or
sunburned bags like the Herefords.

Though it didn't sound as romantic as "cowboy" or as funky as "cowpuncher," I told Mick that I would call him a cowman. He explained further that cowboying was mostly a job. A guy did his work and got a paycheck. Then he was done. But before a cowman could even think about a cow, he had to think about the land and what he and the land could provide: water, grass, hard work, and good luck. Those were the four things on which everything else turns. As his dad used to say when bad weather shut them out of the hayfields, "It rains on the just and the unjust alike." He knew that if he treated the land right and worked hard, the rest would fall into place. He had been at it fifty-two years, nineteen of those on the O Bar Y.

I studied his lean, work-hardened body, still straight-backed and tall. He was just beginning to soften around the middle, and he carried a small belly above his belt. He noticed my examination and said, "Hey, I'm just trying to build a bigger tool shed."

It took me a minute to get the joke, but I laughed and blushed. "You might be a slow learner, but at least you're interested!"

"Mick, what would you do if you didn't have the ranch?"

"Don't know. Die, I guess."

The O Bar Y

When Mick and Margie first looked at the O Bar Y back in the
mid-sixties along with Mick's mother and father, what Margie
saw was the remote location and pole gates that were rigged so
they could be lifted up and pegged on huge posts as the snow
grew deeper and deeper. What Mick saw was the water: the
Green River, Big and Little Twin Creeks and Mud Creek, an
abundance of natural springs, plus multiple artesian wells that
filled the stock tanks in the barns and corrals.

Margie's mind, I'm certain, was focused on how she was going
to raise children and get them to school, while Mick's, I know
because he told me, was on a ranch that had no conflict regarding
water rights. The O Bar Y had first right of use on every source of
water except for the river, but with the creeks, springs, and wells,
Mick wouldn't even have to touch the river. When he saw water,
he saw hay, and when he saw hay, he saw plenty of feed for cattle.
And he knew cows.

I often found Mick standing in front of the big picture windows or the large bay window looking out across the ranch, his

mind working, worrying, and assessing the day's weather and what needed to be done the most. What did he see? Every season was different, each shift of season bringing new, never-before-seen images to savor.

I first saw the O Bar Y on July 19, 1982, when Bill and I drove in from the highway to go up to the Flying A Ranch. I didn't know the boundaries, didn't know which rancher owned what property. All I knew is that we turned off the paved road onto a dirt road that bore no indication of where we were going, no fancy ranch gate to herald anyone's ownership. Mick and Margie's friends had given them a lovely carved wooden sign showing the O Bar Y brand for their going-away present when they left Colorado, but Mick would never let Margie put it up. He didn't want anyone knowing where he lived, and he wasn't one of those big shots who had to boast that he had a ranch. That seemingly small disagreement added one more burr under the heavy saddle of controversies in their marriage.

One reason that Mick didn't want any marker on the highway is that the land immediately adjacent belonged to the BLM (Bureau of Land Management). Once through that public stretch, the road wound down a hill and over a cattle guard into sagebrush pastures owned by the Carney families on one side and the Black Butte feedground, which was state land, on the other. The heavily timbered butte raised dark against the sky was the highest point in the immediate area, a prominent landmark in storms.

From there, the road crossed another cattle guard onto the Buyer land, 120 acres along the river. Mick and his father had built a set of pole corrals there, from which they shipped the O Bar Y cattle in the early days. Then the road forked, the right-hand track going down steeply into the willow bottoms to the bridge across the river, and the left turning into a two-rut track that hugged the ridge and led to the Point, which not only grew abundant hay but also provided additional pasture.

The road coming in from the highway tended to be "slipperier than owl snot" when it rained, but it was nothing compared to the road leading to the bridge, which turned into a vehicle-burying mud pit. The only way I could get through was to gas it, hang on to the steering wheel, and hope that the front tires of the rig could make the bridge approach before the mud demons grabbed me or slewed me sideways into the barbed wire fences on either side. Once I made the bridge and gave a sigh of relief, I had to slow down my heart and the vehicle to creep with caution onto the ancient planks. I had held my breath that first time that Bill and I crossed the bridge, trying not to look down at the wide expanse of the river so far below. For 165 feet I didn't breathe, and that became my habit. What was I afraid of most? That the old mule-driven bridge pilings would sink, that the wooden trusses and supports would give way, or that the oft-repaired planks wouldn't hold?

On the other side of the bridge, the road grew narrower as it made its way past an abandoned beaver slide stacker that had been in constant use during the years when the hay was put up with horses. The road cut the huge river meadows, with their snaking ribbons of irrigation ditches, in two. Wire stack yards dotted the meadows, some emptied of their wealth of bales, and some still holding old hay from years past. There was a gate, then a small bridge with no sides crossing Little Twin Creek, a stream that had "some of the best fishing in the country," according to Old Tom Astle, who had been born with a fly rod in his hands.

From the rich brown loam of the meadows, the road turned into thick black soil along the gigantic hand-hewn log cow barn and multiple pole corrals. Here, too, stood a series of twelve-foot-tall windbreaks to shelter the cattle during storms. Then the road curved past an artesian well that ran fresh water into a glistening round stock tank that remained constantly full. The overflow ran down a ditch into the creek, thence into the river a mile away. From there, a steep hill with a big gate at the top guarded the entrance into the homestead: an architectural miracle of a hand-built log horse barn, an old chicken house that was no longer used, an outhouse and the small cabin that became my abode, the newer home that Mick and Margie had built, the storage shed and two-bedroom cookhouse, several equipment sheds, a shop, and a bunkhouse.

The larger yard housed a hitching post, a line of vehicles both old and new, woodpiles, diesel fuel and gas storage tanks, stacks of lumber and other building materials including spools of wire, a fence post treatment plant, and many piles of what most people would call junk, but Mick called them the "gold mines" because there was always something there that he needed when he was fixing machinery. In the smaller yard around the two houses, a wood-and-wire fence protected Margie's carefully nurtured aspen trees, a few pines, and some flowerbeds. The only thing that gave the place a sense of belonging to the modern world was the huge new satellite dish on the side of the house.

When one left the O Bar Y homestead to head upcountry, there was the choice of turning left once through the gate to go down to the lower BLM leases, straight ahead past the Haley meadow and into Schwabacher's cow camp on the Quarter Circle 5, or across the dump pasture on the trail that led up to the School Section (640 acres of state land), and from there into a half-section (320 acres) of pure heaven on Beaver Creek, and from there on into the 8,000-acre Forest Service lease.

By the time the fall of 1983 rolled around, the O Bar Y had made indelible marks on my mind and heart. I had learned the property boundaries and the cattle trails and the irrigation ditches. I had pulled the baler over many acres of meadow and ridden across many miles of sage. Some evenings, when I wasn't too tired, I joined Margie on her daily walk down to the Point and back. Some mornings, at dawn, I would jog to the river alone, or with Brandy on a lead, simply to hear the great channel of water sing its song and listen to the bird choirs tuning up. I had learned the names of all the horses: the mules Tom and Molly, the Clydesdales Donnie and Clyde, the old Percherons Nell and Bell, the young Percheron-Arab crosses Jack and Jill, the retired teams Stubby and Dick and Pat and Mike, and the long line of saddle

horses: Blue, Poco, Dancer, Jake, Keno, Wink, Rastus, Booger Red. I
had memorized the identities of some of the cows, which Mick
dubbed with whatever name came to his mind, appellations like
"Knot Head," "Society Red," "Croppy," "Bulldozer," and "Snot Nose."

Margie had tried to convince Mick to use numbered ear tags
on his cows and calves so that they could identify them and
mother them up more easily, perhaps even trace the bloodlines,
but Mick stoutly refused. "Hell, if I can't tell one cow from another,
I don't deserve to own them." When I asked him how he could tell
them apart, he looked at me like I wouldn't know my own children
if I had ever had any. "When you look at them long enough and
pay attention, how can you not know?"

I would never have the same kind of intense affinity for cattle,
but I knew that I was falling in love with the land. I had promised
myself when leaving the Northfork of the Flathead River in Montana that I would never again allow myself to fall in love with a
place, because leaving it behind when I moved was entirely too
painful. I had not allowed myself to fall in love with the cabin that
Bill and I had lived in outside of West Glacier, nor the piece of
land we took care of in the Bitterroot Mountains. I knew better
than to fall in love with Snook's place or the Flying A, since I was
only a short-term resident. But after almost a year of walking on
and exploring every nook and cranny of the O Bar Y, the siren
call of love echoed again. Wasn't it okay for me to love this piece
of land? After all, I was with Mick, and Mick said he was never
going to sell out, never going to leave.

The Fall

My twenty-ninth birthday snuck up from behind and blew past like a dust devil. I found a note in my diary, scribbled in Melody's handwriting, accompanied by a frowny face: "Melody *vamonos para* Arizona!" None too happy about leaving, she headed back to school.

A heavy frost hit in early September. The snow that followed brought the cattle down out of the high country, all but the bulls, which had gone into bachelor mode after the breeding season was over. It was too soon to have the cows home, but trying to convince them to go back up on the forest when they knew that winter was right around the corner was fruitless. Luckily, Mick had all the hay taken up off the Haley meadow, so he simply opened the rest of the gates between the cows and the O Bar Y, and they came trailing on in with slick, fat calves at their heels.

Light snows fell and melted. The daylight hours when we could be in the fields decreased, and we were still a long way from being done with the haying. Mick grew grouchy, and Margie more reserved. She was counting the days until they could ship the calves. Then she could collect the check, do the books, pay off the accumulation of stacked-up bills, including my monthly pay, and head for warmer Arizona. I no longer came in for lunch, but took a snack with me and rode the tractor long into the evening, until the dew point dropped and made the hay too tough to bale.

The thermometer registered zero one day during the third week of September. On October 1st, the three of us rode in the rain up on the forest looking for the missing bulls and some steers. We rode again two days later, this time in snow. By the middle of the month, the impending doom of winter convinced Margie to leave for Arizona, taking her Australian shepherd Cisco with her, but leaving behind the cute but obnoxious barking cock-a-poos, Tigger and Bandit. Mick still swathed through snowstorms, trying to at least get all the tall dried-on-the-stump grass knocked down so that the new grass in the spring could grow unimpeded. I pulled the baler home one evening to gas up the tractor, and Mick told me to park it. The hay was too old and rank, with little nutrition left. All the protein, vitamins, and minerals had been sucked out by the cold nights and hard winds. The far meadows stayed studded with bales so soggy with moisture that they became impossible to pick up. They fermented and swelled to the point that Mick couldn't jam them into the chute of the stackliner.

At the end of October, Mick and I trailed the yearlings over to the Black Butte Ranch scales. Before Margie left, she and Mick had argued about shipping the pasture cattle. Mick wanted to keep all the calves and winter them over and sell them the next year. That didn't make sense to Margie. Mick wanted to keep the heifer calves and pick out the best as yearlings to build a new herd. He wanted to see how it might pencil out to keep over the steer calves and sell them as long yearlings. He had plenty of old hay to feed out. She kept trying to tell him that the O Bar Y couldn't survive without a big dose of income. He had shouted at her, "Then sell that no-good piece of desert down there in Arizona." She had countered, "I'm not selling my ranch to keep you from going under."

At the Black Butte Ranch, Mick and I met the Carneys' new hired couple, Chuck and Janet Davis, and their school-age children, daughter Tobi and son Chad. Of the seventy-seven heifers we trailed over, seventy of the heaviest to hit the scales went on the trucks. The cattle buyer, Merv Bumgarner from Nebraska, offered fifty cents a pound with a two percent shrink. Mick had hoped for a higher price. I worried that the calves weren't good enough. They were prime according to Mick, but he didn't have any bargaining power. With the weather getting colder every day, the heifers would start losing weight. I said he should do whatever he thought was right.

Mick nodded his head. Merv wrote him a check for $24,706. That, along with the $6,981 that Ross Calvert had paid Mick for pasturing 206 yearlings, 35 pair, and 6 bulls, was the O Bar Y's total earnings for the year. I thought it was a heck of a lot of money. "Not if you consider the deducts." I asked Mick what that meant.

The mortgage payment would take more than half of it. Then there were monthly bills, Melody's tuition, feed, supplies, and vet bills. Not to mention property taxes, liability insurance, and health insurance. Mick called it the never-ending nightmare; that was why Margie spent so many hours tearing out her hair trying to get the books to balance.

When Margie had given me my wages, I had asked her what Mick and I should do about buying groceries or paying bills, because Mick didn't have a checkbook. She told me that all the bills would come to her in Arizona and that Mick could write a counter check on the local bank at any place in Pinedale, if I could get him to go into town. She didn't think that Mick or I would need any cash, but I didn't tell her that Mick had promised to take me to a movie. "The damn money," Mick said. "It's always about the money. One big goddamned stumbling block."

After Margie left for Arizona, the O Bar Y seemed to take a huge breath and sigh with relief, like letting the air out of a big balloon that had been blown up near to bursting. That evening, I sat down on the living room floor not far from Mick's bootless

feet to watch television. Mick poked me with his toes. I made a
half-hearted tug on his leg. Pretty soon we were goofing around,
trading affectionate slaps, acting like a couple of kids with too
much energy. Then we tumbled into each other's arms like teenagers
whose parents were away on vacation. If I had been concerned
about Mick's affection or his intentions for me, those worries
seemed foolish now.

I still kept all my belongings in my cabin, but I began to stay
in the main house at night, not in Johnny or Melody's room but
with Mick in the queen-size bed. I decided to be wanton, but not
wicked. I left all of Margie's things in place, and I didn't take her
portrait down from the wall. I had no right to change the Buyer
household, one that harbored years of togetherness and memories
worth preserving. Plus I had all the reassurance I needed when
Mick snuggled me in his tight-muscled arms.

One foggy but snowless day, while I puttered in the kitchen, I
heard a knock on the door. It shocked me; rarely did anyone come
to the ranch. Mick was in the bathroom, so I bustled around the
corner to see who it was. I stopped in my tracks with my hand
outstretched to turn the doorknob. There stood Bill: big, broad-
shouldered, in a buckskin shirt with a hunting knife on his belt,
his hair blown about his head. He had his handsome face turned
to the side as he took off his gloves to check on Wraitheon, the
Appaloosa he had tied to the hitching post. When he turned back,
I still had not moved except to lower my arm. His dark hazel eyes
glowered, and his lips were set in a hard line beneath his mustache.
His beard carried a scrim of frost from his breath. He looked like
Blackbeard's ghost. I had not really talked with him personally,
one on one, all summer or fall. When we had chanced to see each
other during those months, other people were around. Now the
kids were gone, Margie was gone. Mick and I were alone on the
ranch. What did Bill want? Had something happened to his
mother or his dad?

I swallowed hard, put the dishtowel I was holding over my
shoulder, and opened the door. He asked for Mick before I could

say hello. He acted like he didn't even know me, so I followed his lead by telling him to please come in, that I would get Mick.

I called through the bathroom door: "Mick, Bill's here." I went back into the kitchen and stayed there. Mick came out, fastening his belt. He looked at me leaning on the counter but didn't stop. He went right to the door. I could hear Bill's muffled words, but he was keeping his voice low. Mick said that he would get his coat and hat.

Mick walked through the kitchen to the laundry room and came back through shrugging on his heavy coat, his hat on his head. This time he didn't look at me. The front door slammed. I peeked out to see them walking down the road toward the cow barn. Wraitheon had his head high and his ears perked watching them go. I sat in a chair by the bookcase where I could look out the big picture window.

What if Mick never came back? What if Bill came back without Mick, swung onto his horse, and rode away? Should I do something? Should I follow them and demand to know what was going on? Should I call someone? Who would I call? Was I being a stupid nitwit? A scared and foolish child? I sat there wringing the dishtowel, tying it in knots and then untying it again. I sat there a long time. It was cold outside. What were they doing? Had they gotten into a fight? Were they both down on the ground bleeding to death?

Wraitheon swiveled his head to stare out past the horse barn. I waited and watched, straining my eyes to catch a glimpse of Mick's black hat. Then I saw them coming through the gate, Bill politely holding open the big poles for Mick to pass through and then re-hooking the horseshoe latch. I bolted back into the kitchen.

I heard their voices outside the front door, but I couldn't understand anything they were saying. I heard Bill's gruff "huh," his command for Wraitheon to move forward. Mick came back inside. He walked past without looking at me to put up his coat and hat. He came back into the living room, sat down in his recliner, and turned on the television. I stood before him, the poor dishtowel still being mangled in my hands. I asked him

what Bill had wanted. He said, "Nothing" and flipped through
the channels.

That was ridiculous. I insisted that Mick tell me what Bill
had said.

Mick looked up with an unfamiliar expression in his eyes:
Extreme frustration. Intense anger. Bottled rage. "He warned me
that you were a man-killer, that you were prone to act nice and be
sweet until you went for the throat." I started to laugh. Nothing
had ever sounded funnier to me. Really? Mick loved to tease,
loved to joke around. This had to be one of his practical jokes.
"The son-of-a-bitch invited me to go elk hunting with him."

More of a naïve idiot than a man-killer, I told Mick I thought it
was great that the two of them could get to know one another.
Mick put down the remote control and stared at me. "I may be
dumber than a box of rocks, but I'm not that stupid." What? An
invitation to go elk hunting was not a suggestion to get together
and do guy stuff. It was a threat. I didn't understand. Mick said,
"Two men go into the woods, both with rifles, but only one of them
comes out." Oh. My bubbling joy from the previous days of loving
fizzled out like an open can of cola. I trudged back into the kitchen
to start supper. Mick brooded all evening and stayed quiet for days.

Bull elk on the Black Butte feedground

Mick with Tammy on the feed sled at the elk feedground

Mick driving Donnie and Clyde in to pick up a load of hay

Mick driving the mules Tom and Molly below the horse barn

The O Bar Y Ranch in spring

The O Bar Y ranch house

Mick sitting on the tongue of his hand-built salt wagon with Sam

Margie and Smoke

Mick on Amigo

Mick

Old Tom Astle, Laurie, Mick. Photo by Joan Wagner.

Laurie and a sleepy-eyed Brandy after a hard day of work. Photo by Mick Buyer.

Laurie on skis near the Haley cabin (between the O Bar Y and the Flying A Ranch). Photo by Lucy Fandek.

The grave of Alexowna Hill above the Green River on the O Bar Y ranch

Easing into Winter

Not long after that, on a snow-filled day, we heard a vehicle coming in from the river, its engine roaring in low gear, low range, to get it up the steep hill past the barn. "Now what?" Mick turned away from the weather channel's ongoing report.

I looked out the window. I didn't recognize the rig.

The passenger left the gate open as the vehicle came toward the house, the driver steering with care across the tracks that marked the yard. The cows, hearing the engine and figuring it was time to get fed, gamboled up from the pasture to follow the noise. I spotted them and threw open the door, saying to Mick's Australian shepherd–dingo-cross cow dog, "Sam! Get 'em out of here."

He raced past the incoming truck toward the cattle like a demon with his tail on fire. I jogged after him to close the gate. As I passed the truck, I held up my hand in greeting, and when the driver said, "Hello there," I recognized him as a hand from the Bar Cross who had expressed an interest in me. I smiled, but kept on to help Sam get the cows out of the yard. The guy hollered at my back, "Sorry about that."

It took Sam and me more than a few minutes to convince the cows that they were not getting fed and that they had to return to the snow-covered meadows to pick along the irrigation ditches for grass that had escaped the swather. By the time I had closed the gate behind the last feisty holdouts and called Sam back from his task, the truck had turned around and was heading back out. I reopened the gate and held it for them to pass through. The man didn't stop or slow down, but he smiled and waved, as did the other three men with him, one up front riding shotgun, and two in the back in the super cab. They all wore hunting garb.

When I puffed back into the house, I asked Mick what the visit was all about.

"Nothing." He stayed intent on the TV.

"You're always saying 'nothing.' They must have come here for some reason."

"Said he wanted permission to take his hunters up onto the forest to look for deer. He's got enough deer on his own side of the valley, so I told him no. Besides, that's not the kind of deer he was looking for."

I caught Mick's play on the words "deer" and "dear," and said I hoped he had been polite. He hadn't been. He had been "god-damned rude," and hoped that "the sniffer had got the hint." When I expressed dismay and said that he couldn't be rude to everyone in the valley who wanted to be nice to me, that I needed a few friends, he replied, "Not that kind of friend."

Jean Senkow had never made it over to the O Bar Y during the summer months for us to go riding together as we had planned, but she called from a pay phone and told me that she would like to ride over before the snow got too deep. Would Mick be willing to feed her horse and packhorse through the winter months? She had a lot of rendezvous and trade show trips planned and wouldn't be home to take care of animals.

Mick said no and let me know he was being polite, but he didn't want strange horses on the ranch because he never knew what diseases they might carry. He had lost one of his best geldings to

strangles—a highly contagious bacterial infection that causes
pus-filled abscesses and swollen lymph nodes that can close off a
horse's throat so that it can't breathe, and it literally strangles to
death. "You don't ever want to have to watch that happen."

Was there anyone else who might winter over Jean's horses?
He suggested that I call Melody Harding. When I phoned, Melody
was agreeable: if we could get Jean's horses to the Bar Cross before
another heavy snowfall, she would be happy to feed them over. I
caught Mick as he was going out the door to check the stock tanks.
"Melody said yes. Now I need someone to haul Jean's horses to
the Bar Cross when she—"

"Oh, for Christ's sake. Yes . . . yes, I'll do it."

The day Jean rode over, she raced a fast-moving storm front.
We stabled her two geldings for the night in the aluminum stock
trailer that served as a kind of quarantine. The next dawn brought
snow. As soon as we gulped some coffee, we secured Jean's horses
in the trailer and pulled out of the ranch, with Mick driving and
me riding in the middle. The slick highway made me hold my
breath and made Mick travel at a snail's pace, but we made it
without incident to the Bar Cross. Mick unloaded Jean's horses
in an empty corral. Melody was not at home, but we wandered
around waiting for her to appear as the snow grew deeper and
the air turned colder.

"Ladies," Mick said, "unless you want to spend the winter here,
too, we'd better get gone." I told Jean she could call Melody later
or give me the care instructions and I would call her. Jean held
on to the necks of her horses and patted them goodbye.

Mick kept his truck in four-wheel drive and used the rearview
mirror to keep an eye on the slip-sliding empty trailer. He heaved
a relieved sigh as we turned off the highway. When we reached
the O Bar Y headquarters, Jean's partner, Sam, had already arrived
to take her home. Since the storm was gaining strength with every
passing hour, they didn't stay, not even for a cup of tea. But when
Jean hugged me goodbye, she let me know that I could always go
with her and Sam on the rendezvous trail to sell my beadwork. I

pondered that window of opportunity but told her I was set to stay with Mick, at least for the winter. Mick decided to stay grouchy and uncommunicative, so after supper I built a fire in the stove in my cabin and sat at the rough-hewn table to write by kerosene lamplight.

I scribbled a letter to my friend Ken Iddins, asking him whether he could find me a pistol, something easy to shoot, something light enough for my small hand. Ken had known Bill when they both served in Vietnam as Navy medics. He had stayed in touch over the years. A gun collector of some renown, he knew firearms better than anyone. I didn't tell him why I needed a pistol. If he asked, I would say that I wanted it for an emergency in case my horse got hurt when we were riding on the forest.

When I returned to the main house, Mick had just slammed down the phone.

"I hate that goddamned contraption. If it's not delivering bad news, it's somebody who wants something."

Margie wanted him to haul the travel trailer that was parked in town down to Arizona for her. He was going to have to leave the next day if he was going to get it there before the thing snowed in. He groused, "All I do is haul stuff back and forth between here and there. Oh, what the hell. It all pays the same."

I didn't want him to go. I was afraid to be alone on the ranch, but if he had to leave, could I please have the keys to the house? They didn't have keys to the doors. They never locked doors, not on the house or the outbuildings, not on the vehicles or equipment. I didn't understand. With fading patience, he explained that in the country, they left doors unlocked in case people got stranded and needed to get out of the weather or use the telephone. Someone might have to borrow a vehicle or a tractor. I asked, "Like who?" He sighed and said, "Hunters, snowmachiners, another man's hired hands, folks who get lost. Why are you asking me all this?" I said, "Never mind."

But it worried me. Even if the door was locked, Bill could easily break a window and open it from the inside. I couldn't walk into the entryway without seeing his visage as it had been when he came to see Mick. It unnerved me during the day, but at night, when I tiptoed through the house to use the kids' bathroom so I wouldn't wake Mick, it terrified me. I refused to give in to the fear. I made myself look right at the window. Shaky-knee relief surged when nothing was there but my own reflection.

Most nights I didn't go back into Mick's room. I slipped into Melody's bed, listening for the sound of hoof falls or snowshoes or skis. When Mick asked me where I had been, I replied that I couldn't sleep, that my back ached or I was restless. I never told him about my concern that Bill would slip down some night from the Flying A to do us in. This way, if he came, Mick and I would be in separate beds. Even while my rational mind said that Bill would never do something horrible—he wouldn't risk the chance of being put in prison—my irrational mind still remembered his temper at his worst. I sensed that he was biding his time.

When Mick pulled out for Arizona, he told me that he would be back as soon as he could. He was going to drive straight through, drop off the trailer, turn around, and head right back. I thought that he at least ought to get something to eat and stay the night, because he shouldn't drive if he was tired.

"Yes, mother," he teased. "Are you going to be all right?"

Of course, I fibbed. I had the dogs and the telephone.

Going Out

The pistol Ken had ordered for me came in the mail. I unwrapped it in my cabin and held it in my hand: a .38/.357 with a shortened barrel and a sweet ivory handgrip, cold, heavy, and hard. Ken had included a note that read: "Here you go." He had taken the liberty of adding a hand-tooled holster and a shell holder. I would have to take the gun in to the sheriff's office and get it registered and buy a box of bullets in town. It was against the law to send ammunition through the mail.

Though I had learned how to shoot, both rifles and pistols, on the Northfork of the Flathead, I still didn't feel entirely comfortable with guns. Bill had criticized my weak eye and unsteady hand, but even if my aim had never been the best, it would be good enough at close range with a target as big as a man.

Mick returned from Arizona looking like a bedraggled Bedouin who had lost his horse. I told him to get inside so I could feed him, but he said he wanted a bath first. He had not slept at all, though he had pulled over on the Navajo reservation for a few hours. Some "son-of-a-bitch" had woken him up by trying to steal the trailer, so Mick had started the truck, jerked it in gear, and "knocked the sorry shithead on his butt." I didn't understand why he hadn't stopped to call the police. He snorted. "On the reservation? What good would that have done?"

I thought he would have at least stayed one day to visit Melody, but he said that she was in school—or at least he thought she was. He said he "hated it down there in the country of nothing but piss-burnt flats." He pulled a silver-bead and tiger's-eye necklace from his jacket pocket and said, "I got you this."

Before I could even thank him, he was stripping off his dirty shirt and unbuttoning his jeans as he headed for the bathtub. When I asked him what he wanted to eat, he shouted, "Anything." I heated up some canned vegetable beef soup, and we sat down together at the table. When I told Mick that I had an appointment to go see Doc Johnston the next day, he surprised me by saying he would take me to town. I said that I also needed to register a pistol that Ken had sent me.

Mick squinted his eyes as he crumbled crackers into his bowl and asked why I needed a pistol. "Well, you've got a .45, a shotgun, a couple of .22s, a .30-.30, a .30-.06, and that other thing with the huge scope that's covered with dust."

"That big-ass caliber is enough for elephants or rhinos in Africa. Some 'mighty hunter' Margie leased the cookhouse to left that here as a gift, but no one needs something that big for deer, elk, antelope, or moose. You didn't answer my question."

"I just thought I should have my own pistol."

"Fine, but I watched you practice with your .22 all summer. You didn't make much of a dent in the gopher population."

I laughed. "I can't bear to kill them so I only try to scare them."

"Into what? Leaving the country?"

"But you're a good shot, right? You can teach me."

"Dead-eye Mick. I never miss. You'll do fine. We'll set up some targets out at the dump."

Mick sat like a restrained wolf in the clinic waiting room while I saw Doc Johnston. Thyroid fine. Cholesterol elevated. Blood pressure still high. Anemia a tad better, but still holding sway. Doc Johnston studied me. He wanted to know if I was eating enough red meat and if the birth control pills were working. I didn't tell him, just as I had not told Mick, that beef didn't agree with me. I was used to eating wild game. The pills seemed to slow the bleeding, but the pain was as bad, if not worse. He scribbled out a prescription for a pain reliever called Motrin and handed me another prescription for a different kind of birth control pill. He admonished me to come see him in the spring. He knew I probably wouldn't get off the ranch once the road snowed shut.

"That Mickey being good to you?" He adjusted his glasses. I told him yes.

"Glad you're on the pill?" He grinned as he winked at me.

"Mick said he doesn't trust them." I winked back. "He still uses condoms. Said he doesn't want any more 'buns in the oven.'"

We laughed as he walked out into the waiting room with me to shake Mick's hand. When Doc asked him how his knee was holding up, Mick replied, "Wish I could wrap it tighter with baling wire." Doc wanted to know if he was staying off it and taking the anti-inflammatory. When Mick waved his hand at the air, Doc Johnston said, "Play now, pay later. You take care of yourself, or this gal will be digging you an early grave."

Mick and I stopped by Falers for groceries, filled my prescriptions, and bought a box of .38 shells. When I registered my pistol, my hand shook as I signed my name.

"What are you planning to do," Mick teased, "shoot somebody?"

He took me out to lunch at a café. A couple of neighbors stopped to clap him on the shoulder and shoot the breeze, but he gobbled down his burger and French fries like a starved dog. "Let's get home," he said. "I'm about as uncomfortable in town as a virgin in a whorehouse." I asked him how he knew about whorehouses, and he told me to remind him, that he would tell me sometime.

Melody Harding called the following week. Richard was taking her to Big Piney to see *Indiana Jones and the Temple of Doom*. Did we want to go? "Ah, hell," Mick said, "I guess I promised you, didn't

I. That means I've got to put on my good boots. Tell her we'll come and meet them at the Bar Cross."

At the Bar Cross, the four of us crowded into one pickup for the trip to Big Piney. The darkened theater. The warmth. The popcorn. Mick with his arm around my shoulder. He and Melody engaged in a competition to see who could eat the most red licorice. Melody won: two bags to Mick's one. The movie was fast-paced excitement, but totally unrealistic. When we finally reached home again after midnight and stepped in the door, Mick let out his characteristic huge sigh of relief.

What had he been doing, holding his breath all night? Hadn't it been fun for him at all? He said he would "rather be drug through a knothole without grease."

Melody called me often after that. We talked on the phone, sometimes for hours. She and Richard were having troubles. He worked in town, and she worked at the Bar Cross. They never had any personal time together. He wanted her to slow down and pay attention to their marriage. Melody had said to him, "You mean besides milking, separating, churning butter, cooking, cleaning, riding my horses, and feeding the cows?" She laughed that she shouldn't joke about it. He was serious. He wanted more intimacy. He had suggested last fall that they take a day off and go up to the lake, so Melody dutifully packed a picnic and took a horse blanket to sit on. "How did that go?" I asked.

"Not so good," she laughed. There wasn't anything to do after they ate, so Melody climbed some rocks, then told Richard that she wanted to get home and check on the dog.

Richard called me next. Melody had told him I was easy to talk to. He explained that Melody had never wanted to be married, but she also didn't want a bunch of randy cowboys bugging her all the time. She figured that being married would keep the boys off her back, so she married him. He loved her for her incredible beauty and all her accomplishments, but they had about as much in common as a real bear and a teddy bear, with Melody being the real bear. I listened to his complaints. He ended by saying that he knew not to make her mad, because the last time he had pushed too hard, she had taken all his stuff and thrown it out into the yard. He loved the way she cooked and kept the house, but he wanted a closer connection. He wanted to know if I would ask her for him.

I wished Richard well, then waited for a while before I picked up the phone again.

Mick wanted to know what was going on. I hushed him, explaining that I was busy walking the balance beam between being a friend to one and a confidante to the other. When Melody answered the phone, I told her what Richard had told me. She wanted to know why she should bother. She didn't understand what the big deal was about sex anyway. When I mentioned orgasm, she laughed and said, "Explain that one to me." Melody tended to sleep in the recliner because her back hurt all the time. Richard told her that if she wouldn't try to hand-stack a thousand bales of hay in one day, she wouldn't hurt so much. She told him she wasn't going to give up being foreman on the Bar Cross, and in order for the men to respect her, she had to outwork them. She didn't know what she was going to do. She never should have married Richard in the first place.

When I told Mick what was going on, he said that Richard had had his hands full from day one, but that they would work it out. I wasn't so sure. Like Mick and Margie, they were both staring at the same handwriting on the wall. But whose translation was right?

Thanksgiving

As the snows continued, I began noting the number of bales we fed to each category of cattle: so many to the calves, to the cows, to the bulls; so many to the horses and to the elk. The short days had the look and feel of another tough winter. We needed to use care early on, or we would run out of feed before spring. Because of my continuing health problems, I quit eating beef and asked Mick if he would shoot an elk for me. He said he had not "drawn down on an elk for years." When I asked why not, he explained that he had a "strong kinship with the herd on the Black Butte." I was sorry I'd asked, but he added, "I have a landowner's license. Let me see what I can do."

The first time we saw a bunch of elk come down out of the high country and gather around one of the haystacks trying to get at the feed, Mick said, "Let's go," and grabbed his rifle. We jumped into the pickup and made it down to the Mud Creek crossing as several hundred elk thundered past. Mick stepped out of the truck, leveled his .30-.30, and dropped the lead cow. The rest of the elk turned sharply and headed down a fence line, swam across

the river, then thundered en masse up the other bank and over
the sagebrush flats to the sheltered timber of Black Butte.

Mick and I gutted out the elk. We left the pile of intestines for
the coyotes. When he pulled out the internal organs, we saw that
he had shot the cow right through the heart. He dug out the bullet
and gave it to me. I was impressed. He said, "So were the big shots
in the Army. That's probably why they stuck me on the front line."
I thought that something to be proud of, but he said there was no
sense in shooting if you couldn't shoot straight. Did I want the
cow's eyeteeth? Yes, I would use them with some beads to make a
necklace for his mother for her birthday. Mick carved the ivories
out of the cow's jaw and commented on how worn they were. "I
think I shot the oldest cow elk in the valley." That was good. That
meant she might not have made the winter, and it didn't look like
she had a calf.

We threw the quarters into the back of the truck, and Mick
strung them up in the shed next to the cookhouse. After the
carcass had hung for a week, I spent several days butchering out
the meat, labeling each white-wrapped package as steak or stew
meat. I ground the scraps to make sausage and put the bones out
by the dump for the ravens, magpies, and howling coyotes.

When Thanksgiving time drew close, I asked Mick what he
wanted to do. We had bought a frozen turkey earlier in the fall,
and I had promised to make all the fixings and bake some pies.
Did he want to invite anyone to come and join us? Not really. Did
he think we should invite Bill? He looked at me over the top of
his reading glasses and set down his stock paper. "That's not the
smartest thing I've ever heard."

"I don't know. Maybe if we befriend him, he will know that we
care about him and he won't . . . " I didn't finish my sentence.

"Won't what? Be crazier than a loon?"

I choked, then swallowed. I reminded him that he had promised
me we would always try to be friends with Bill. "Oh, hell, if it's
what you want, I'll try."

We drove up to the Flying A one afternoon in mid-November, barely making it through the deepening snow in the leafless aspen groves. Bill didn't come to the door when we drove up, but he came to the knock. We stood on the porch as Kyote whined and licked my hand, while a new German shepherd puppy gamboled about barking.

"Makwi, hush!" Bill commanded.

I knelt to receive a face washing of doggy kisses so that I would not have to meet Bill's eyes. Mick spoke for me: "Laurie said she would make Thanksgiving dinner, and you'd be welcome to come and join us." I added that we would eat early enough in the afternoon that he could get home before dark. Bill said that his friend Taos was due in any day, and that he would be staying awhile. "Bring him, too," Mick said. Bill nodded.

As we drove back down the mountain, I said, "He didn't make that easy, did he?"

"Why would he?" Mick said.

"Why is it that men never want you until you're gone?" I replied.

Two days later, Bill called the O Bar Y. When I answered the phone, he asked me to come up for a visit. Gooseflesh riddled my arms, but I said all right. As I fixed noon dinner for Mick, I told him I was going to ride Brandy up to the Flying A, and asked if that was all right with him. He stayed quiet, but then said, "It's your funeral. But I don't get it. Why do you keep doing this? He doesn't want to be your friend. He only wants to get you back."

"Well, I'm not going back. I'm only going up for a visit. Maybe it will help."

"Suit yourself."

The day turned cold and stormy. Bill brought out a tarp to throw over Brandy's saddle. I touched the lump in my coat pocket for reassurance. He fixed tea, and we sat at the kitchen table to watch the snow falling. We talked with ease about his mother and father, about our friends Sam and Jean, Ken, Brent, Len and Lisa. We talked about a new technique he was perfecting for his antler

artwork and new handles he was making for his hand-forged
knives. He showed me the stack of deer and elk hides he had
tanned and smoked. We talked about everything except the O Bar
Y, except Mick and me. As dusk began darkening an already dim
sky, Bill said that he would go partway with me.

We rode in silence as a full moon appeared on the horizon. On
our way down the Little Twin draw, we spooked a bunch of elk
out of the aspen trees. They scattered in a thunder of flying snow.
Bill counted seventy-four head. I counted seventy-six. He said that
we would split the difference and call it seventy-five. He handed
me a package and told me to give it to Mick. When I asked what it
was, he said, "Elk steaks." I thanked him for a nice afternoon.

He touched the edge of his fur hat and wheeled Wraitheon
away. Brandy nickered as the Appaloosa disappeared in the
gloom. I turned him toward the O Bar Y and nudged him into a
lope. When I reached home, after I had turned Brandy loose, I
held the pistol in my pocket as I walked to my cabin. There I stored
it in the original box and put it on a shelf. I stomped the snow off
my boots on the porch. Mick came to the door to meet me. He
looked relieved and said he took it as a good sign that I had come
back. I handed him the package. When he asked what it was, I
said I thought it was a peace offering.

When Thanksgiving Day arrived, I set the table for four. Mick
watched football on television while I basted the turkey and made
potatoes, gravy, rolls, and green peas with onions. I kept watching
the clock. One slipped past and then one-thirty. Then two.

Mick commented that if Bill and Taos hadn't come down off
the mountain by now, they weren't coming. I picked up the dishes
and silverware that I had set out for Bill and Taos and put them
away. My pouting silence told Mick the state of my heart.

"You have to give it up and let go." He held a turkey leg in his
hand like a gavel.

"You mean like you have with Margie?"

"That's different, Gallantry. We have kids. We're in business
together. You can't divide up a ranch like you can the silverware."

The pumpkin pie tasted like ashes in my mouth.

A few days later, Bill wrestled the Scout down off the mountain with Wraitheon tied to the back bumper. He parked his rig out at the highway and then rode back up to the Flying A. I saw him go by both times, and though I waved from the window, he didn't stop. I did not understand, I would never understand, why we couldn't be friends.

Margie and Melody called on November 29th to wish Mick a happy anniversary. It was their twenty-fifth year of marriage.

An Attempt at Christmas

At the beginning of December, John Fandek called from the Bar
E Bar with bad news: Bangs disease had been discovered in the
Carney cowherd, and the federal vet had issued an order that all
their cattle were to be branded with a "B" on the left cheek and
then shipped immediately to Idaho Falls for slaughter. The ranch
was quarantined, John told Mick, complete with warning signs
on all the gates. All adjoining ranches, including the O Bar Y,
were required to test for the disease. That's all John knew except
that he was sorry about the problem and the resulting inconve-
nience. Mick set down the phone like a man who had been given
a death sentence. "I don't want any goddamned federal agents on
my ranch."

I thought it important to find out whether the O Bar Y cows
were infected, but Mick accused me of being "an innocent" who
didn't know what I was talking about. I hadn't been around in the
late thirties and forties, when they were "driving cattle into bulldozed pits and shooting them" because of an epidemic of hoof-
and-mouth disease. I reminded him that John had said Bangs

disease, not hoof-and-mouth. Plus, no one would just show up and shoot his cows. "Want to bet?" he said.

The federal vet Doug Woody called next. On a bitter below-zero day, Mick and I gathered everything bovine into the corrals by the cow barn. One by one we ran the animals up the alley, slapped on a numbered tag with rubber cement, and pushed them into the squeeze chute for Dr. Woody to draw a blood sample before turning them into an adjacent corral. The noise of confused cattle coupled with human tension created a turbulent atmosphere. Exhausted, we went up to the house for hot drinks and a warm, dry place for the vet to run the blood samples. He found only one heifer with what was called a "tighter reaction," a residue of the disease probably left over from her Bangs vaccination when she was a calf, but there was no way to make sure. Mick had only two choices: he could immediately slaughter the suspect heifer, and that would free the O Bar Y from any further speculation about the disease. Or he could keep the heifer alive, quarantine the ranch for a time, and eventually retest. Mick paced the living room while Dr. Woody packed up his test kit. I started making a much-needed meal.

"All right, damn it," Mick said, "I'll put her down. But not tonight. Tomorrow."

Dr. Woody was required by law to be present at the time of death, so Mick invited him to stay for supper and spend the night.

After breakfast the next morning, Mick and I sorted off the red heifer wearing the unfortunate number that meant her death sentence. We drove her into the barn and into the narrow alley with the head catch. Mick had brought his .45 from the cookhouse gun cabinet, but he had found only two bullets. He had fussed, but one shot was all he would need. Then it would be done.

The vet stood in the half-open doorway, which let in just enough light to see by. Mick climbed up on the board alleyway, pulled the pistol from his coat pocket, and put in the two shells. He looked at me. Nervousness spiked from his eyes, and his hand shook. I nodded. He aimed at the back of the heifer's head and the shot exploded, echoing off the barn walls. The cattle and horses in the corrals outside burst into motion. The dogs erupted into barking. But the heifer didn't fall. She stood there flinging her head at all the commotion. Mick had either closed his eyes or jerked his arm upward when he fired. He couldn't try again, so I tugged on his coat sleeve, and he clambered down, saying, "God-damn it to hell." I didn't give him a chance to say any more. I pulled the pistol from his hand, climbed up the boards, placed the gun on the heifer's axis joint as Bill had taught me, and pulled the trigger. This time she went down, dead before she hit the ground. Again the horses and cattle outside milled in startled confusion, and the dogs set up a stark howling.

"What now?" Mick choked out. "Can I at least eat her?" Of course, but first Dr. Woody had to fill out the last of the paper-work, and Mick would have to sign it. Then the vet would be on his way.

After Dr. Woody pulled out of the ranch, Mick and I put a rope on the heifer and pulled her into the open with the four-wheeler. We gutted her quickly in the gathering brightness of the day as the blood froze on our hands. Then we strung her up by her heels to let the meat cool. We still had dozens of bales to feed and waterholes to open. By the time we came back down to the barn in the early evening, the heifer's hide had frozen to her flesh. We would have to thaw the entire carcass to skin her.

"To hell with that." Mick got his reciprocating saw. He cut her into quarters as shavings of red flesh covered the snowy ground like sawdust. We hauled the four large pieces into the unheated cookhouse and set them on the kitchen table. Then we piled the guts and head and lower leg bones onto a little trailer and pulled what was left of the red heifer over to the dump. Mick grabbed her head by an ear and gave it flight. At least the coyotes would feast.

Mick's fifty-second birthday, December 12th, arrived with no letup in the arctic blast of cold air and wind. The T-bone steaks, mashed potatoes, peas, coleslaw, and spice cake I made for his celebratory dinner helped lighten his dismal mood, but it was the arrival of two of his friends that brought him out of his "the whole world's against me" dumps. Mike McClain and Mike Hammit zoomed into the ranch on snowmachines with a bottle of whiskey to toast "old Mick." Then the stories flew, and the laughter gained in volume. Near midnight, Mike and Mike decided to head home before their wives called the sheriff. They offered to take the stack of pre-wrapped and ready-to-mail Christmas packages I had waiting by the front door. They would drop them at the Cora post office, where the postmistress, Joanne Ludwig, kept a small tin of my money to pay for postage.

A week later, with the temperature registering –22, Mick and I cut and decorated a big pine tree for the living room. Margie, Melody, and Johnny were coming home for Christmas. I packed a small suitcase. Mick wasn't happy about my leaving. He was going to miss me, but I told him that I would send postcards with a secret message. Every time I wrote "How is Brandy?" it would mean "I love you." He needed to be with his family without having me constantly underfoot. And I needed to see my folks, too. I manhandled my station wagon through the mounting snowdrifts to the highway, then finessed the icy roads to Rock Springs to catch a flight to Colorado Springs, where my mom and dad would pick me up and take me home with them to Woodland Park.

On New Year's Eve, I called Mick. He was home alone. Johnny had gone back east, and Margie and Melody were "gone galli-vanting in Jackson Hole." What had I been doing without chores to take care of? Eating my mom's great cooking, seeing family friends, going to the movies, shoveling snow from the driveway. He had racked up the same experiences: eating Margie's cooking, seeing the kids, watching TV, and shoveling snow. Mick asked, "Was 'Sandy-balls' good to you?" I had received a set of saddle-bags, a pair of jeans, a velour blouse, and a portrait of Brandy that Mom had painted. He had received the usual pocketknife, work gloves, flannel shirts, and new winter cap, but his favorite gift by far was the photo album I had given him full of pictures of him, his horses, and the ranch.

A long silence ensued. Was I coming back? Yes, if I still had a
job. It was waiting for me, and so was he. Great! I needed the
money. I had tallied up my wages, plus the income from writing
articles, plus the beadwork I had sold. After I had done my
"deducts" for postage, long-distance phone calls, Brandy expenses,
and all the miscellaneous stuff, I still had almost a thousand
dollars. It was more money than I had ever had in my life.
"Good!" Mick said, "How about a loan?"

"Sure, as soon as I get back. And listen to this: Did you know
that when you love something, the pursuit of it shapes your life
and gives it meaning so that you don't depend for your entire
significance on someone else? That reminds me of you. Of you
and your love of the ranch."

"Pretty deep," he teased.

"And there's something else, too. This comes from *The Women's
Room* by Marilyn French. She says, 'loneliness is not a longing for
company, it is a longing for kind. And kind means people who
can see you for who you are, and that means they have enough
intelligence and sensitivity and patience to do that . . . One needs
some reflection from the outside to get an image of oneself.'"

"You'll have to run that one by me again," he said.

What it meant was that I loved him because of the reflection
of myself that I saw in his eyes. That he helped me see myself as
strong-minded, open-hearted, kind, caring, beautiful, and worthy.

Sassafras

Alone on the O Bar Y, Mick and I grew even closer that second winter of 1984. From sunup to sundown, we did everything together, seldom more than a room away from each other. We ate together, showered together, slept together, and worked together. While Mick spent countless hours plowing snow, tromping feed trails with the snow-cat, fixing equipment, shoveling roofs, and doctoring cattle, I went cross-country skiing or worked with Brandy in the corral.

January brought us deeper snow and unusual cold. Our feeding rounds took us most of every morning as we harnessed and hitched one of the teams and loaded hay on the sled to feed a couple dozen horses, over a hundred head of cows, and about that many weaned calves and six bulls. With home chores finished, we headed out on the two-mile sled-packed trail to the Black Butte feedground to put out hay for more than five hundred head of wintering elk.

Late that month, with the temperature at −20, the game wardens came to do a head count. They came up with 410 cows, 11 bulls,

20 spikes, and 99 calves. "Good god, man," one of the wardens said as he slapped his frozen hands together, "how do you do this every day?"

"Got to justify my wages," Mick said. "And it beats being a desk jockey pushing around a pencil."

Despite the dense cold, I loved that part of the day best. Our journey took us over acres of snow-buried meadows across a narrow bridge on Little Twin Creek. We traversed another long stretch of meadow before reaching the huge wooden bridge that spanned the snowed-over Green River. One day, on the ice below the bridge, we spotted a cow elk lying near the willow-edged bank. It was odd to see a lone elk midwinter. When the team and sled clattered onto the bridge, the cow spooked, struggled heavily to her feet, and tried to run. She was hurt. Mick thought that her hip was broken, probably crippled by some hunter. He clucked to the team, urging them to trot away from the poor animal struggling in the snow. I looked back to see her stumbling on three legs, her right hind leg stuck out at an awkward angle from her rump. I watched till she was out of sight.

We breasted the ridge above the river and continued on across the sage-covered pastures, now buried under several feet of snow. At the feedground, I opened the extra-tall gate for Mick to pull the team and sled in alongside a haystack. Mick tossed sixty large bales down to me, and I stacked them in even rows. We pulled out of the stack yard without an elk in sight. As we straightened out the team to feed, the herd poured down off the aspen-timbered ridges. The elks' squeals and barks broke the morning silence as they whirled and ran. Mick drove. I kicked off flakes of hay. We watched the elk jostle each other to get to the best feed.

Here, too, were crippled elk: a big old bull with a front foot gone that had returned to the feedground year after year, and a cow with her front leg gone below the knee. Despite the grievous injuries the elk suffered at the hands of incompetent hunters, they still trailed into Black Butte. They knew where to find hay during the long winter months. The lone cow on the river ice had been trying to make her way back to the herd. With the snow so deep, she couldn't travel the last mile.

I wrapped the baling twine in a bundle and hung it from the sled upright. Mick had saved several flakes of alfalfa to take a little feed to the cow if she was still there. He doubted that we could save her, but said we would try. As we crossed the bridge on our return, Mick threw the hay close to the spot where the cow had bedded down. Her tracks led upriver around a willow-covered bend. Would she come back? She might, but it was a wonder the coyotes hadn't gotten her already.

The following day, I squinted through the falling snow to see the elk as we crossed the river. She was not there. But Mick noticed her tracks, and the hay was gone. She was hiding under the bridge. Mick again brought hay, and this time he threw it close to the bridge abutment where the cow would have shelter from the wind. As we turned the final curve for home, I spotted a dark speck against the green hay on the white snow.

I tired of calling her "that crippled cow." She became part of our daily ritual, so I searched for a name. Sassafras seemed fitting: feminine and spunky. She proved to be a very savvy elk. Her hiding place under the bridge with a snow-free bank of earth kept her relatively protected. The river ice stayed solid under a thin blanket of snow so that she could travel short distances without exhausting herself. If harassing coyotes came, she could back up against the bank under the bridge to protect her flanks. We worried about moose horning in on her daily ration of hay, but none seemed inclined to visit that stretch of river.

When Sassafras heard the team and sled approaching, she hobbled out and stood until we returned with her hay. She seemed to know that she would come to no harm. On the rare occasion when a snowmachine passed over the bridge, she panicked and tried to run. If I came on horseback to get the weekly mail at the highway, she peeked out with caution. She knew my voice when I talked to her. If I crossed over on skis, she learned not to be afraid as long as I didn't stop.

In the evenings after supper, Mick and I watched the miniseries *Centennial*. Mick thought the "old boy Pascal" acted a lot like my mountain man. I reminded Mick that Bill wasn't mine anymore. Mick wanted to know whether Bill had been my "first." No, my fourth. Why? Because I had been restless and dissatisfied. I kept searching for something in men that wasn't there. Had he had any girlfriends other than Margie? He had had a crush on a girl who lived on the ranch over the hill from the Buyer Ranch outside of Fairplay. His mom had teased him that if Carol would have him, they could combine the ranches and own most of the county. But he was too shy to even say hello, let alone ask for a date. He never got a chance to do more than daydream. He liked the Neukirch girls, Belle and Violet, who were wild and beautiful, and fine horsewomen to boot. Once when he and the hired man Slim were out riding, they saw Belle and Violet wrangling in a horse herd. Slim teased Mick, saying, "Ride hard and catch one of them." Mick joshed back, "Hell, I can't ride hard!" Slim kicked his colt "in the slats," and Mick followed suit, but as fast as they galloped, the Neukirch gals outran them. He never got to go with one of them. The local bad-mouthers whispered that a line of thievery ran in the clan. His mother only had to tell him once that the Neukirch girls were considered off limits.

Was Margie his first sexual encounter? He teasingly accused me of "trying to pry it out of" him. I apologized, but I was curious. He had had his "first taste" with "a poor little gal" when he was on leave with the Army in Japan. He wasn't proud of that. He had been drunk, and he wasn't proud of that, either. It wasn't even his choice: the other guys had goaded him into it to prove his manhood. If she had told him her name, he didn't remember it. "What was it like?" I asked. It had not been pretty. Unwashed smells. Choking darkness. He had been glad to get out of there.

What about San Antonio, when he was in the MPs? He liked the pretty *señoritas*, but that first time had spooked him off, and he didn't want a repeat performance. What about when he came home from the Army? He laughed and told me I was like "a fly on a cow pie." But I wanted to know everything there was to know about him. He was about "out of skeletons in the closet," but he had really liked a local woman he saw when he was out drinking with his buddies around Fairplay. His mom and dad heard about that, of course, and his dad warned him about her reputation. And? He couldn't just stop a story in the middle. He cleared his throat. "I was lonely, and she was willing. I came down with a case of the clap and had to ask Dad what to do. That was tough, but better to ask Dad than to have to ask the other guys. But it lowered me in Dad's estimation."

Mick's father had said nothing. He merely pointed Mick in the direction of the doctor's office. Later, when Mick apologized, his dad said, "Well, if you're going to dance, you have to pay the fiddler." I wanted to know what had happened to the woman, and Mick said, "She married my best friend, and I stood up for them at their wedding." When I told him that he didn't get much of a break in the heart department, he said, "I've never gotten a break. It's not in the cards." "What happened then?" I asked. He said, "I waited. I kept my lonely to myself."

Hearing Mick talk about his first sexual encounters made me love him that much more because of what he had lost and what he would never know. How much different would his life have been if he had lost his virginity with a hometown girl with whom he had fallen in love rather than an anonymous Japanese prostitute? It was an event that changed forever his impression of women and sex. And it affected all of his relationships thereafter.

In early March, Mick received a long handwritten letter from Margie. She confessed her distress and disappointment that their marriage had come to an impasse. "We only have this one life, this one chance for happiness. I want to set you free to love Laurie with all your heart. She's a good person and worthy of your love." We both cried.

Little Evalyn

April greeted us with other concerns. Three of the cows had died with the brisket, an edema caused by the high altitude. Mick dragged them off behind the John Deere crawler, taking them several miles away so that the coyotes wouldn't be drawn in too close to the ranch during calving. John Fandek called to tell Mick that his calves were dying on the Bar E Bar, and he didn't know why.

The first robin appeared, and then the geese returned, honking over the river where the ice was breaking up, followed by a steady influx of returning animals: snow geese, cranes, curlews, even the skunks. Days of horrible storms were interspersed with days of warmth. Mick began to hitch two teams together, driving them four-up to get the sled through the softening snow crust and the deep mud.

My health had not improved. I tried not to complain. Instead I began keeping track of my symptoms and read *Our Bodies, Ourselves*. I was doing better on the elk meat than I did on beef or chicken. I gave up coffee and cut back on sweets, stopped using Jim Beam as a crutch, and turned to a heating pad for relief. On my bad days, I couldn't walk or stand up straight. When I struggled trying to put on my coveralls and pack boots, Mick scolded, saying he would not allow me to go out. I yelled that he couldn't do the calving all by himself, and that caused him to say, "Want to bet? Who in the hell do you think was doing it before you showed up? Go lay on the couch."

Later he came in to sit by my side. He wanted to know what was wrong, but I had no answer except that I felt stressed out and anxious all the time, like the bottom of the world might drop out and leave me hanging by a thread. Mick said, "Join the club. That's ranching." I confessed that I was counting my blessings: a secure place to live, a good horse, worthy work to do, and a man who loved me. He agreed. He had some news to cheer me up: the blond heifer with a bald face that he had given me as a bonus the previous year, the one I had named Evalyn after Snook's wife, had given birth to a heifer. Mick patted me on the back. I was officially in the cow business. Did I plan on naming her, too? Of course: Little Evalyn.

When the road opened up, I kept my promise to see Doc Johnston. The birth control pills weren't doing me any good. Since Mick insisted on using condoms, I wanted to quit taking them. Doc agreed and asked, "What else?" A nasty rash on my calves. Nothing had stopped the redness and itching. Was it from handling and doctoring new calves? Like scabies or ringworm? Was I allergic to something? It looked like sand flea bites to him. "Have you been to the beach out at the lake?" he asked. I laughed: that was hilarious. He gave me a prescription for anti-itch cream. My blood pressure was still too high, and he wanted me to find some things to do for stress relief. When I asked, "Like what?" he replied, "You're a hot-blooded young woman. Figure it out."

At home I found Mick fuming over an article in the *Pinedale Roundup*. What now? "The goddamned environmentalists and the goddamned logging companies have the Retels tied up in court."

Joe and Stella Retel of Rock Springs had spent many summers on a piece of land that adjoined the Moore ranch. During the time that Bill and I had lived at Snook's on Tosi Creek, the Retels had befriended us. Often inviting us over for supper, Stella always offered me a real bath since I lived without running water and plumbing. I missed her and Joe.

I took the mangled paper from Mick's hand to read the coverage. Distraught, I dusted off Margie's typewriter again. Over the course of several hours, I pecked away, writing and rewriting until I had honed seven long paragraphs into a condensation of the legal battle over the right of way on Retels' private road. "Many of us wonder why timber sales in the Upper Green don't go to local Sublette County loggers, small contractors who would not have the same type of maximum impact as Louisiana Pacific. Why doesn't the Forest Service allow more use of harvestable timber for house logs? Why are people only allowed to gather firewood on a restricted basis? Isn't there a better balance for the land and for the people than what is being proposed? Shouldn't the value of the land and the timber be determined by its meaning to all people instead of sacrificing it to whatever corporation can pay the most?" I ended my diatribe with a thank you to all the people in the county who had sent the Retels money to help them defray the cost of their legal fees and signed, "Sincerely, Laurie Wagner."

Did Mick think that my letter would do any good? Hell no, but if it made me feel better to write it, he said, then I should write away. He asked whether I had had any luck with my magazine articles. Besides the cover photos in *Wyoming Rural Electric News, Cow Country,* and *Wyoming Stockman Farmer,* I had pieces pending with *Beef, Farm and Ranch Living,* and *Horse and Horseman.* "See," he said. "And you didn't know if you had what it takes to be a real writer."

"All I know is that it calms my mind and eases my heart. What helps you, Mick?"

"Snickers. Did you get to the store? Did you bring home any candy bars?"

In May, as the buttercups bloomed and the green grass appeared along with a chorus of frogs, we had a serious wreck with Jack and Jill pulling the wagon. Jill spooked at the canvas-covered John Deere crawler newly parked in the corral. Both horses went berserk, bucking and rearing. Mick had his hands full with the lines, but he yelled "Jump!" to me just as Jill's hind hooves took out the sideboards. I landed on all fours, bolted upright, and then rolled away. Somehow Mick managed to ride out the rodeo and keep the wagon from tipping over. I stood at the horses' heads and held on to their bridles as Mick picked up the shattered wood. "Well, I'll be go to hell in a hand basket," he said. "Now I've got to fix this."

After feeding the cattle, we trundled through herds of returning antelope down to the BLM lease to fix fence. An uncharacteristic roar swooshed over, causing us to instinctively duck our heads. We looked up in time to see an eagle diving in to kill a duck on the edge of a tank filled with melted snow. "That's something you don't see very often," Mick said. "Beautiful, isn't it? But those buggers sure gave us hell during lambing." I wanted to know more about running sheep. He and Margie had tried it early on. The Mocrofts had run sheep on the O Bar Y before he bought the place, but between the coyotes and the eagles and the weather, they couldn't keep enough lambs alive to make it profitable. He didn't miss the sheep, but he missed watching the Basque shearers at work. "Those boys knew what they were doing."

Toward the end of the month, I rode up to the Flying A to check on Bill, but he was not there. I returned the next day, only to find the lodge vacated. I fed his corralled but unattended horses. Later, I received a letter from him with a strange, smeared postmark and a new address, but since it held no hint of kindness or understanding, I didn't reply.

I invested my energies in spring-cleaning the main house and moving my scattered belongings back out to my dusty cabin. In early June, I stayed in the cabin for the first time in eight months. When Mick asked why I was going out there, I replied that I needed to get used to being without him again.

The Second Summer

On June 12th at 6 P.M., Margie and Melody pulled into the ranch. The following day, all of us helped John and Lucy Fandek brand the Bar E Bar calves. Ten days later, on Johnny's birthday, the Fandeks came over, and we branded the O Bar Y cattle using a new calf table. It took six of us an hour and a half to brand 77 calves. The O Bar Y herd had grown to 153 cows and replacement heifers.

Margie and Melody pitched in to fix fence and irrigate. The four of us rode for fun one day up past the DC Bar, around Dodge Butte, and through Sawmill Meadows, where we saw huge herds of deer, elk, and antelope. When my parents came for a short visit over the Fourth of July, Mick took them up on the forest in his wagon to salt the cattle while Margie, Melody, and I rode alongside horseback. On our return, we came through the Flying A. The corrals stood empty, the lodge still unoccupied. My mom asked where Bill had gone, and I said I didn't know. She hoped and prayed that he was happy. She and Dad missed receiving his adventure-filled letters.

Margie bolted in and out, tending to bull buying, banking problems, and various meetings. She flew to see her mother and brothers in Colorado Springs and Denver. She traveled to visit friends. When I joined her in the mudroom one afternoon to help her fold the laundry, she explained that she was trying to stay out from underfoot, to not interfere with the working pattern that Mick and I had established. It was difficult to know where her territory ended and mine began. "We're like the Mormons, only poorer," Margie joked.

"How did Mormons manage to have so many wives in one house?" I asked. My guess was that the husband was never there except to have sex. Then he went off, and the women and their children had to make their own separate peace with each other.

"You and I do great when we're alone," she said. "I'm guessing you and Mickey do fine when you're alone. But when the three of us are together, the tension runs at warp speed. I'm never sure if I should stick around and try to help with the house and the hay or just get out of the way." I let her know that Mick and I appreciated the help, but she said he only wanted her around because he needed another horse and was too homebound to go look for one.

Mick stomped his feet as he came in from outside and wanted to know what we were gossiping about. I said, "You." He washed his hands at the sink, and I tossed him a towel. "What about me? What did I do now?"

"I'm complaining because you won't ride Smoke," Margie said. "I bought him last summer so you'd have a new horse."

Mick said he was no good. Attempting to take Margie's side, I offered that Smoke was stout and handsome, but Mick wasn't going to give an inch. "He's dull. He's got no spark. Not worth a damn for working cattle, plus he hates to cross water. He won't put a hoof in a mud puddle. You ought to take him down to Airy-zony, where he won't have to face a creek or a stream or a slough or a river."

Margie bristled but didn't bark back. She calmly suggested that Mick spend some time with Smoke, but Mick said that he was not going to spend his time fighting with a spoiled horse. He had better things to do!

"Fine! I'll leave this minute, and I won't come back until I've found you another horse." She picked up her purse and keys and hurried out the door. Her truck started. I scolded him. "What? What did I do now? Can't a man even speak his mind?"

Margie returned several days later with a seven-year-old buckskin named Amigo. She unloaded him in the yard. Well trained in the arena, he knew a little about cattle. She only had to give a couple thousand for him. Mick scrutinized the gelding and said, "Oh, hell. Part Arab, but okay, I'll try him out."

Mick saddled Amigo and I saddled Brandy, and we rode out together to put the new gelding through his paces. Margie was waiting on our return. "Like I thought," Mick said, "high-headed and flighty. He can't keep his feet under him in the sagebrush, and he doesn't pay attention." But Margie wanted to know if he reined well and if he could turn fast in the corral. Mick grumbled that he was good enough to get by on.

"If that's the way you feel, I'll take the son-of-a-pooch back," Margie countered.

"Forget it. You already paid for the stumblebum." Mick swung out of his saddle, wincing as his weak leg hit the ground.

"Stick 'Beetle-brains' in the isolation corral." He handed me the reins and stomped off toward the shop.

Margie hollered, "Why don't you go and find the GD horse you want, then?"

"Because I don't have the time!" Mick yelled back.

Why, she wanted to know, could she never seem to do anything right in his eyes? I apologized for Mick. I thought that Amigo was beautiful.

"But Mickey thinks he's brainless—just like me. If I had a brain, I'd leave this snowbound, money-gobbling place for good and never look back."

I volunteered to put the horses up and suggested that we tackle cleaning out the basement under the cookhouse. "Oh, fudge," Margie said. She had forgotten that she had said she wanted to get that chore done.

I helped Margie wrench up the trapdoor, and we climbed down into the dim light from 40-watt bulbs. Blackened cobwebs hung from the ceiling. The dirt floor was damp with moisture. Mold and mildew clung to every box and bag. I pinched my nostrils shut to keep from breathing in the dank air. I saw clothes the kids had outgrown hanging from rods, as well as various sizes of skates, skis, and other athletic equipment, games and toys. Johnny and Melody were gone. They wouldn't be coming back. The sharp sadness in Margie's voice kept me silent. She sighed like a tired horse and said it was time to get rid of all the stuff, to carry it up the stairs into the light of day. Whatever wasn't useful, we would haul to the dump.

As I grabbed an armload of clothes, I spotted Mick's Army uniform, complete with commendation pins over the front pocket. Margie said to leave it. She was sure that Mick still wanted it. I held out a leather bomber jacket that had a map of Korea on the inside. It had belonged to Warren, a Navy pilot who had wanted to marry her. She held it in her arms. She should let it go, as well as her old party dresses. She picked up a yellow dress with a fluffy fur collar, the dress that had first drawn Mick to her at the bar in Antero Junction. She told me to toss it, and all the rest, too. She had outgrown them, and they were out of style anyway.

I asked her where Mick was stationed when he was in the Army. Basic training at Fort Bliss. Then Korea. That's where all the boys went. Where was he stationed in Korea? She didn't know. He never talked much about it. She only knew that he was on the front lines for a while. Why did I ask? I said that I was curious because my dad had flown over Korea and Vietnam a few times with his unit.

Bit by bit, we accomplished the onerous task. Mick pitched in late in the day to help us haul truckloads of stuff to the dump. I started coughing and couldn't stop.

"What's wrong?" he asked.

"I think I'm allergic to mold and mildew."

"You want to take the rest of the day off?"

"The day's over, you nut. And, no, I don't want time off. I want to help Margie fix your supper."

"Am I in trouble again?" He pulled the braid at the back of my head.

"Always."

Mick's Demons

I went to bed early, but came down with a serious fever and bronchial infection that laid me low for weeks. My cough disappeared, but I found it difficult to get a good, deep breath, and I tired easily. We finished cleaning out the cookhouse and made some progress in the hayfields. I came in one evening from baling to find Mick hollering and Margie almost in tears.

"Why can't you get it through your thick skull that I am not going to sell out! Not now. Not ever. Especially not to some asinine developer who will cut the O Bar Y into pieces like a piece of meat."

"All I said was that I stopped in Jackson Hole and spoke with a realtor. I—"

I interrupted to say that I was done for the day. The tractor had run out of gas. I was going to bed. I grabbed an apple from the fruit bowl and left them still arguing. I had fallen asleep in my cabin when Margie burst in the door, barefoot and wearing a short sleeveless nightgown.

"He's going to kill me." She was shaking all over.

I tried to rouse myself from the bed. What was going on?

"It's Mickey. He . . . "

She started sobbing, holding her hands to her face as if that would keep the sound from spreading. I closed the door and took her over to the bed, telling her to crawl in and get warm. I started to light my lamp, but she said, "No, don't do that. I don't want him to know where I am."

Where was he? What had happened? I sat next to her on the bed. She was shivering so hard, her teeth chattered. She had gone to bed and was almost asleep when Mick had come in the bedroom and grabbed the pillow off his side of the bed. "He said . . . " She couldn't finish the sentence. I held her hand and kept saying that it was all right. I wouldn't let anything bad happen to her.

"He said . . . he hated . . . my fucking guts. He said he was going to . . . I don't know. I don't know. He stalked out of the room, and I jumped out the window to come over here."

"You jumped out the window?" It wasn't a far drop to the ground, but far enough, especially in a nightgown and bare feet. She nodded her head and clenched her fists and held them close to her mouth as if she were trying not to scream.

I kept telling her it was okay, as if I could convince myself as well as her. She had never seen him like this before. She had never heard him sound so angry, so furious. He had never used the "F word" in front of her before. I pulled on my jeans and shirt over my long johns and told her to stay there, that I would go see what had happened.

She didn't want me to go over to the house. Something was wrong; something was terribly wrong. I argued for her to just stay there and stay warm. If there was anything she could do, then I would come and get her.

"You can't go over there. Laurie, what if he hurts you?"

"He's not going to hurt me, Margie," I said, even though I wasn't sure about that. I slipped out the door, closing it softly behind me.

There was a half-moon rising, so I had no trouble making my way to the darkened house. The dogs remained quiet; they knew me. I stepped inside and said, "Mick?" but there was no answer. I walked into the living room and was headed toward the bedroom when I heard muttering. I stopped. "Mick?" I said again.

He was lying on the couch, fully dressed, including his boots. His body was rigid, and he held his hands clenched on his chest, but his arms kept jerking as if he were trying to break free from some invisible bonds. The pale moonlight showed that his eyes were open and his mouth was moving, but he could neither see nor hear me, though I said his name a few more times. He was seeing and hearing something else. He mumbled, his voice deep and angry, and his teeth gritted so tightly I thought he would break his jaw.

"What is it?" I asked. "What's wrong?"

He spoke a bit more clearly, and I leaned closer to hear. "God-damned sons-of-bitches. I know you're out there. I hear your fucking boots in the snow. Come just a little bit closer so I can blow out your fucking brains."

I stepped back, not scared, but in disbelief. I had been in this situation more than once with men I had known who had been in Vietnam. I had watched Bill outmaneuver his demons for eight years. But Mick had been too old for Vietnam. I had never thought about Korea. Why hadn't I thought about Korea? Mick wasn't with me at the O Bar Y in the spring of 1984. He was on the front lines in a bunker during one winter in the early 1950s.

What should I do? I had no training. I had never been able to do much to help Bill. But I knew that I couldn't leave and go back to my cabin. I couldn't send Margie over here to her own house. She would be petrified. I didn't think Mick would do something bad, something dangerous, but I couldn't be certain. I had heard enough stories . . .

I tiptoed into Melody's room to get a pillow and her bedspread and blanket. I laid them on the floor next to the couch. I knelt down and spoke in a whisper to Mick, hushing him like a mother would talk to a child having a bad nightmare. He raged and then he quieted, his face breaking out with sweat, his eyes wide and unblinking. I tried to take his hand, but he jerked away, cursing.

But I stayed. I knelt there and I prayed to whatever God would listen. I kept my voice soft, speaking the way that Mick spoke to his horses when they were spooked. Finally, after the longest time, I felt him relax. The entire room eased as if something awful and evil had slipped out through the moon-bright window. Sam came and whined to be let outside. I rose and opened the door, and he raced away, barking into the night. Far off, the coyotes howled.

"What?" Mick sat up halfway.

"Nothing. Just coyotes. Lie down. Go back to sleep."

I placed my palm against his cheek, now cold as marble, spiked with the first stubble of new beard. I put the blanket over him and took his sweaty hand. I lay down on the floor and pulled the bedspread over me. Eventually, I heard Mick breathing deeply and then snoring.

I didn't think I had let go of his hand, but I must have, because when I woke to sun streaming in the window, he was gone. I looked in the bedroom and the bathroom, the kids' rooms and the laundry room. His coat and hat were gone. I put the pillow and blanket and bedspread back in Melody's room, and I took Mick's pillow back into his bedroom. I opened the drapes and made the bed where he and Margie had slept for so many years. I put on a pot of coffee and walked over to my cabin. Margie was awake, but still snuggled in my bed. Was she okay? Yes. She knew that Mick was gone. She had heard the three-wheeler start. I suggested that we go over to the house for coffee.

"Good thing there's nobody here to see me," she joked as she picked her way across the wet grass and rocks in the yard. "They would wonder what I was doing coming out of your cabin barefooted with only my nightgown on."

We attempted laughter, but settled for a couple of big sighs. We sat on the couch, and Margie drank coffee while I made myself some tea. She wanted to know whether he was all right, and I said I thought so, that he had finally slept. What had he said to me? Nothing at all. He just seemed upset. Tears crept into her eyes again. "He didn't say anything about me, about hating me?"

No, nothing about her. The tension we had all been under had finally gotten to him. I wondered where he had gone. Margie said, "To the woods. All these years when he's taken off like this, I ask him where he's been, he tells me he goes to the woods to get his head on straight again."

I nodded. I understood more clearly why Mick didn't want to be in town or around a lot of people. Like Bill. Like the other ex-military men I had known who tried to outrun their demons. Margie wanted to know whether he was still mad at her. I didn't think he was mad at her. He was mad at the world, at the stupid, pitiful unfairness of it all.

When Mick returned, he didn't come to the house. He slipped into his shop and stayed there. I let him be, but at suppertime I went to find him. He unscrewed something from the vise and set it on the workbench. He offered a small "I'm sorry" smile. He wanted to know why he had been sleeping on the couch and I had been sleeping on the floor. I didn't know what to say. Did he not remember what had happened? I shrugged. Margie had supper on the table. Wasn't he hungry? He followed me out the shop door and up to the house. He took my hand. He said, "You looked so beautiful and peaceful lying there this morning, I didn't want to wake you."

"That's okay. I was worried about you. What did you do all day?"

"Sat on a log. Threw stones in the creek. Whittled on a stick. Sometimes I just have to get away from everything."

He was quiet at supper. His face was calm and his hands were steady. I was glad he had the woods and that he didn't turn to the bottle or to drugs or to violence when the demons slunk out of hiding. He and Margie had a little spat. Nothing serious, but she said she would sleep on the couch and Mick said no, that he would. Then Margie said, "You sleep in the bed. You're used to that. I'm used to the couch." She added, "I don't know why I'm trying to sleep in the bedroom anyway. You snore too much."

We laughed together, and some part of each of us that worked to try and make a team fell back into place.

Korea

Praying that the episode had passed, I didn't tell Margie what had happened with Mick that night. If Mick had never told her, then I didn't feel it was my place to reveal those things about his past. But later, when Mick and I were working alone in his shop, I asked him to tell me about Korea. He set down the sledgehammer he was using to pound on a tractor part. Why? Because I wanted to understand what had happened to him. When he said it wasn't important, I disagreed and said that it was.

He hesitated. He had never told anyone. Not really. Not his parents, or his sister and brother-in-law. Not his friends in Fairplay when he got back from overseas. Never Margie or the kids. Why not? Because he didn't want to talk about it, and he still didn't. He motioned for me to follow him outside. We sat on stumps in the sun. He took out his pocketknife and started whittling on a stick.

If he wanted me to stay with him, then he was going to have to tell me. Life was hard enough when I knew what I was dealing with. I didn't want to be caught with him in a bad state of mind and not know what was going on. For starters, I knew that he hadn't wanted to go. He confirmed that. Who would? It was stupid. His dad could have gotten him out by claiming a hardship situation. He could have said that he needed his son on the ranch. But he had Slim to help. And Slim had been in World War II. Mick's sister Arlene's first fiancé had been killed over the English Channel. Walt, too, had "fought the Japs."

Mick wasn't drafted, but all the other guys were signing up, so he told his dad that he had better go too. His father took him down to the Army recruiter to talk about the cavalry unit in Colorado Springs. The guy promised Mick that was where he would go, so he signed up. But the recruiter had lied. They told Mick later that the Army didn't want any damn cowboys in the cavalry. They didn't want any "yahoos from the sticks telling them what to do with their horses and mules."

So Mick didn't get in the cavalry. He got "cannon-fodder training." His mom and dad took him to the train. Crying women. Screaming kids. Soldiers everywhere. His dad said, "Keep yourself straight and do what they tell you to do, and then you can come home again."

Mick had never been on a train before except to go to Denver. When the recruits got to the base, the building they were told to go to was locked. They all stood around cussing and shivering. Finally, Mick used his pocketknife to jimmy a window so they could get inside. The next morning, some sergeant busted in, yelling at them for no good reason. Mick, the only one with cowboy boots and a hat, stuck out like a sore thumb. The sarge tried to scream Mick into getting angry, but the man didn't have a chance. Slim had been yelling at Mick his whole life. He was used to verbal abuse.

He aced the groundwork and guns in basic training. That was easy for him. He guessed that he had done all right on the tests because the "bird-shit-on-the-shoulders" guys wanted to send him on to school to be an officer. He said, "Thanks, but no thanks. I'd rather be a private in the rear ranks."

I didn't understand Mick's reasoning. If he had had more
training, he might not have had to go to the front lines. But he
explained that he didn't want to be giving orders to anyone. He
didn't want any responsibility. He gave up whittling and flipped
his knife end over end to stick it in the dirt. He retrieved the
blade and repeated the action.

He asked me if I had ever been on a ship, and I said yes, five
days, from Honolulu to San Francisco. He told me to think of an
entire battalion crammed together puking on each other and
fighting the drizzling shits. Nothing but garbage for uniforms.
Boots that didn't fit, that wore holes right through their socks
and blistered their feet into bloody stubs. None of the men were
prepared. The officers shoved them onto trucks. All of them still
sicker than dogs. Whenever Mick got the shakes, he would think
of the high country and the big bucks he used to hunt. That
helped, especially once they started seeing bodies stacked up
alongside the road half-buried in the mud. That did little to boost
their confidence.

They unloaded at a base camp with a mess tent, but then the
"upper echelon" loaded them up with ammo and sleeping bags
and told them to start walking. They went for miles into the
mountains. "Everything around us blown to shit. Colder than
a witch's tit." Some of the southern boys couldn't stop shivering.
The ones from the cities couldn't even stay upright on the uneven
ground. At the line they told the men to count off. They sent some
east and some west. Mick got east and was glad because of a steep
ridge, and that's where he headed. He didn't stop at the first
bunkers along the way like some of the guys who thought they'd
be better off being closer to the trail back to base camp. Not him.
He wanted to be as far back in the boondocks as possible.

No one told them what to expect. Not one word. Mick ended
up in the last bunker on that side of the line. When he climbed
the tall ridge, he could see the sea way off in the distance. And
to the north a deep valley, and then high up on the other side
the Chinese.

Hearing the mortars coming in was the worst—the awful whining before the explosion. Never knowing where they were going to hit. The guy they put in the bunker with Mick lost it. He wouldn't even get out of his sleeping bag. Mick did jumping jacks and push-ups to stay warm. He started digging a trench in front of the bunker to have a place to walk to keep from freezing. The other guy kept saying, "Buyers . . . Buyers . . . I'm dyin' here," and kept pissing in his "fart sack" until his legs froze. When he quit talking, Mick walked down to tell somebody. They came and got the guy in a jeep. Mick never saw him again, never knew whether he made it.

Then he was alone, and that was all right by him. Nights were terrible. He could hear boots squeaking in the snow and hear "jabber," but he couldn't see them. On the bad days, Mick couldn't hear himself think for the firing. Then it would go silent, and that was worse. That and having nothing to eat but frozen C-rations and a little square of chocolate. No latrines, and nothing to use to wipe his butt. No way to bathe unless he scrubbed his face with snow. Even then, the lampblack stayed stuck in his pores.

The only time away from the line of fire was when he hiked down to base camp a couple of times to try and get a hot meal. That was a laugh. The cooks couldn't keep the food from freezing. Once he stopped to take a leak in some trees and found a dead man. He didn't know why, but he took the ROK ring off the Korean soldier's hand.

It didn't help to go down just to have someone to talk to, because then he saw the casualties going out and new guys coming in. He didn't want to talk. What could he say? How stupid it was? So he stayed at his bunker the whole time. A hundred and twenty days. At least there he could try to keep safe. So many didn't make it. Not because they got shot, but because they froze up or starved out or shit themselves to death. He wasn't ashamed to say how terrified he was. Every minute. Always listening. Always looking over his shoulder. Never sleeping. But he wasn't afraid like some of the guys. He wasn't afraid of working hard to dig that trench.

Hell, he'd been digging ditches all his life, and that's what saved him: when a mortar came in too close, he dove into the pit, and his only injury was some shrapnel below one knee. He lost so much weight, he couldn't tighten his belt enough to keep his pants up. When the "uppity-ups" trailed his platoon out, they trailed the new guys in. Mick never looked up. He didn't want to see their questioning eyes. Nor did he say anything. What could he say? He focused on the ground and kept moving.

But he didn't get to come home. The "bigwigs" sent them on a boat to "Ja-pan for I & I." Not R & R, rest and relaxation, but I & I, intoxication and intercourse.

With a half-hearted laugh, Mick flipped his knife shut and shoved it into his pocket.

Then home? Nope, back to "Frozen-Chosen" for more maneuvers. They were supposed to bust through the front line and push it farther north to the river. That's how he lost hearing in one ear— from being under the tanks when the guns went off. The all-out push wasn't successful, but the "powers that be" gave them all the Bronze Star anyway. Then he got to come home for a short leave: a couple weeks. No one said anything. No one asked him anything. He went to work every day, like always, with Slim yelling at him and his dad grinning around a wad of Red Man in his cheek. His mother gave him a hug and baked him a cake. Before he knew it, he had to go back and finish out his time, but not overseas again. The "top brass" offered to put him in the MPs at Fort Sam Houston in San Antonio. That sounded good to him. He stood guard at General Wainwright's funeral. He got serious about drinking. It helped take the edge off. No counseling. No help. There was no such thing.

When he finally got out and went home to the ranch, he stayed out a lot with the guys drinking. The next day, when he couldn't eat breakfast and puked over the edge of the hay sled feeling like shit, his dad just grinned and said, "We'd better get one more load. Put it on for tomorrow." Mick guessed that his dad thought that hard work would straighten him out. And eventually it did. He had seen a lot of drunks around Fairplay. He knew the stuff would kill him. After he married Margie, he knew he had to stay away from the bars. That's why he didn't like to go out or be around a bunch of people. They lied. They couldn't be trusted. At least when he was on the ranch, he didn't have to keep looking over his shoulder. Nobody was shooting at him here.

Mick snorted and stood up. He stretched and resettled his hat on his head. When I asked why he had never wanted to talk about it before, he said, "What good does it do to spill your guts when no one cares?"

We walked over to the house. I asked to see his photos. Mick pulled things out of his top dresser drawer: several pictures of him and the other guys in their parkas, some Korean currency and military scrip, his Army recommendations and his discharge papers. He sat at the table drinking iced tea while I put together a photo album for him. I took the Bronze Star and the commendation ribbons off his moldy uniform and put them in a nice box along with the ROK ring. I asked for the world atlas, and he pulled it off the bookshelf. I found Korea. He showed me where he had been. We sat hand in hand on the couch. He talked long into the night, but there were many times when he stopped, shook his head, and refused to say more. He had been nineteen. It changed him forever. And for what? The war had been so stupid. All that time and money wasted. All the lost lives.

A Night Out

Mick's war experience gave him an extreme hatred for and distrust of the government and the military. His time in the Army exacerbated his childhood paranoia about people and urban areas. Steady and kind in his own environment, Mick was from the old school. He had inherited a life on the land and the role of a rancher. He had found salvation in hard work, because when he was working, he didn't have to think about the past, and when he got done working, he was too tired to think. The hard work on the ranch gave him a purpose and a focus. And it helped him sleep, except when his arms went numb from pitching too much hay or his legs cramped up with charley horses from riding too far or snowshoeing too many miles.

Mick didn't relish a fight, any kind of fight. He might battle the weather or cuss out a piece of broken-down equipment or raise his voice at Margie out of pure frustration, but he wasn't likely to clobber someone for no good reason. He did tell me one time that he was fine as long as no one tried to back him into a corner. Now Margie had him in a corner. He couldn't divorce her without losing his ranch and cattle—and he had already lost one ranch, his childhood home, through a series of sad misfortunes with his sister and brother-in-law. That had made him bitter. Korea had made him bitter. The fact that Margie had given up on him and left him made him bitter. I was the only sweet thing in his life except for Snickers candy bars and Cokes, his drugs of choice. He couldn't divorce Margie because he couldn't afford to lose the O Bar Y, not financially and not emotionally. It was all he had— and he was all I had.

We stuck it out, determined to keep the ranch going. The three of us tried hard not to get in each other's way or hurt anyone's feelings. I did believe that we would find a way to work things out if we continued to keep each other's best interests at heart. Then Margie upset our delicately balanced triangle by talking to the realtor in Jackson Hole again. An appraiser showed up on the O Bar Y in early August, which sent Mick into another tailspin. In mid-month, the realtor brought in prospective buyers, and that choked Mick into a stupor. We had a tough night. The fragile tripod threatened to topple and fall apart. I stayed by Mick's side until dawn. The hardest part for me, I told him, was that I had no input and no control. The O Bar Y was not my ranch, nor was my marriage at stake. All I could do was stand aside and watch, to be there to help pick up the pieces.

The day before my thirtieth birthday, I quit the hayfield to go into town. I didn't ask for permission. I told Mick that I was taking two days off to celebrate by getting a motel room and going out to eat. Margie was going to come in, and so were Melody and her new boyfriend, Frank. Did he want to join us? "I'd rather be shot," he said.

When I registered at the motel, the owner knew my name. My questionable reputation as Mick's hired help had preceded me. She looked askance, as if she were going to refuse me a room. Instead, she asked me a lot of questions. Then, before she handed me my key, she told me that they didn't allow female guests to have gentleman callers. I nodded that I understood, but when I

left the office straight-backed, I put a definite swish in my hips. I
should have been offended, but I wasn't. How small-town hilarious
that she thought I might use her establishment as a place for
illicit business.

I spent the night eating junk food that I bought at the conve-
nience store across the street: potato chips, Cheetos, Cokes, and
candy bars. I sprawled out on the bed like a complete decadent
and watched movies on television. I loved using a bathtub and a
toilet that I had not had to clean. The following day, I strolled
around town, visited the stores, stopped at the bank and the
library. I even spent some of my hard-earned money to have my
hair done. I read a lot, wrote letters, and scribbled page after page
in my journal. Excited about a night out, I dressed in a silky white
flowing skirt and blouse. High heels felt foreign on my feet, but I
smiled at the sexy pose of my three-decades-old self in the mirror.

Margie picked me up at the motel, and we met Melody and
Frank at MacGregor's Pub, the nicest eating establishment in town.
We drank wine. We ordered escargot and steaks with grilled
mushrooms, baked potatoes with lots of butter and sour cream.
We selected something outrageously sweet for dessert. We
laughed until we were sick and then ordered after-dinner drinks
and coffee.

The Stockman's Bar had a live band playing, so we gravitated
there. Frank danced with all of us and told ridiculous jokes: What
do you call a girl with fat calves? Rancher's delight. What do you
call a girl with a sunken chest? Pirate's treasure. It was easy to see
why Melody enjoyed the company of the tall, handsome, blue-
eyed young man who had come from Washington State to learn
how to tan hides from Bill and stayed on in the area. It was also
easy to notice how Margie sparkled in the presence of someone
who talked to her, listened to her, and paid her sincere compliments.
Way past midnight, I bid all of them goodnight and stumbled through
my motel room door. I fell into bed feeling like a bad dream.

The next day was no better. I spent the morning soaking in a
tub of steaming water with my eyes closed in hopes of getting rid

of my hangover. I waited until the last minute to pack up and check out. The proprietress, standing primly behind the counter with her hands folded, scowled at my squinty red eyes and shaky hands. Did I know that there were only two reasons for a younger woman to be involved with an older man? I blinked at her question, but I didn't bother to respond because I knew she was going to have her say whether I wanted to hear or not. One was looking for springtime, and the other was looking for Santa Claus.

I had to hold my breath to keep from laughing before I managed to get through the door. Once outside, I allowed the hysterical guffaw stuck in my throat to erupt. I forced myself to get behind the wheel of my car before I went back inside to see whether she wanted to trade jobs with me, maybe shoveling manure or doctoring scour-sick calves.

I drove the long miles back to the ranch with intense slowness. Mick, greasing equipment in front of his shop, eyed me like a cow with scabies when I got out of my car. I didn't want him saying I told you so. I waved and smiled and kept on walking.

After putting my belongings in the cabin, I soft-footed it into the main house. I found Margie holding her head on the couch. We looked at each other and said, "Damn!" Well, I said, "Damn." Margie said, "Darn!" I suggested we keep our misery to ourselves. She volunteered to tough it out on the baler if I would go turn bales. I felt certain we would survive, but Margie wasn't so sure about it as she got her hat and gloves. I followed her outside into the hot sun.

The dry wind felt like sandpaper on my face, and every time I bent over to move a bale, my stomach turned upside down. Hours later, Margie and I met back at the house, both silent and grimacing at the dismal prospect of fixing supper. Mick's wry smile told me he was gloating, but he knew better than to say anything about our discomfort. He did say that the Retels had come by to bring the writing desk that I had asked Joe to make. "We barely got it through the door," he said. "It's a heavy beast."

The three of us tromped out to my cabin. The handcrafted pine desk sporting seven drawers took up the entire wall under the west window. "Joe said he tried to get you knotty pine without the knots, but they didn't have any at the lumber yard. You owe him $140." I smiled at the old joke, and said I was surprised at the low cost. "He said pay him for the materials; the rest is a gift from him and Stella toward your writing career."

"That's a big investment, which means I'd better get busy on some more articles."

"You'll have rainy days," Mick said.

"And snow," Margie added, "coming way too soon."

For the next thirty days, we suffered through too many rainstorms and cranky temperaments, but the baler count rose to 10,996, then to 13,410. In mid-September it rained all night, then snowed all day until eight sloppy inches covered the land. Hundreds of snow geese landed on the meadows. We hauled hay up to the cattle on the forest to keep them from breaking down the gates and coming home. Losing time against the impending autumn, Mick sighed that all we could do was keep on trying.

"What do we do when the 'try' runs out?" I asked.

"Don't know, Gallantry. I never quit, even if I bellyache a bunch."

Wink

Melody and I volunteered to help Schwabacher's crew gather cattle. I rode Brandy, and she rode her Thoroughbred barrel horse. Wink had a gall starting on his thin-skinned side where the cinch had rubbed him, so Melody double-padded him under the saddle, offsetting the blankets to cover the sore spot. She also cinched him fairly loose.

Mick warned her to tighten it up. She shouted, "Dad, I'll be fine" as we rode out. She was glad to get away from the house. It was like walking on eggshells around her parents. All they did was argue. Problems, problems, problems. Why couldn't they just be nice to each other and enjoy life? I was sorry about the tension, but I didn't know what to do to make things better.

We found different bunches of yearlings in the coulees and draws in the Miller Section and the School Section. We pushed them steadily toward Schwabacher's pens miles away. A sullen steer cut back at a bridge on a creek, and Wink turned sharply to go after it. As if in slow motion, I saw Melody's saddle slip. I saw her fly sideways through the air. I watched her land heavily on her arm and shoulder. I spurred Brandy over in time to see her stand up, yelling, "Where's Wink?"

I had not even paid attention to her horse. We spun in circles searching and caught the back end of him trying to gallop with his hind hoof caught in the stirrup of the belly-turned saddle. "Oh, no! Oh my god!" Melody tried to run after him, holding her hurt arm. I slid off of Brandy and stopped her, telling her to slow down and wait, that we would only spook him worse if we ran.

We walked together across the sagebrush, following Wink's dim trail of dust. We found him down, lathered white. Melody began to cry. I had my hands full trying to hold on to Brandy, who kept shying away from the thrashing horse on the ground. One of Schwabacher's old cowboys galloped up and vaulted off his horse. "Goddamn you girls!" He had known there was trouble as soon as he saw the horse loose on the horizon. He told Melody to step on Wink's neck to keep his head down. He cut the cinch and carefully pulled the horse's torn and bleeding leg out of the stirrup. He threw the saddle aside. "Stand back! See if he can get to his feet."

Melody had a death grip on the roping rein she had unhooked from one side of Wink's bit. But when he finally found the courage to rise, he didn't attempt to run. He stood there quivering, his right hind leg hanging. "Stifled." The cowboy said it like a cuss word, like it made him sick. He pointed at Melody. "You take that goddamned roping rein and burn it!"

Melody slumped with her face against Wink's neck. And I stood there stupidly staring at the ground, holding on to Brandy like he, too, might fly away over a ridge and be hurt. "Don't you have a brain in your head? If you used split reins, chances are he would have stepped on one of those. That would have stopped him or at least slowed him down. That sissy piece of shit hanging around his neck didn't do doodledy-squat, now did it?"

The old guy spat. Then he swung up on his gelding, wheeling

the horse sharply. He told Melody her horse was done. "Walk him home. Then come back for your gear." He rode off, mumbling, "Stupid . . . worthless . . . women."

Screw him, I thought. I wished I'd been packing my pistol. Not for Wink, but for that old fart. Melody might have made a mistake, but he had no right to talk to her that way. I hated him. I hated all men. I hated military men. I hated mountain men. I hated ranchers and I hated cowboys. I hated the way all of them used us and worked us to death and then made us feel worthless.

We walked back to the ranch together, Wink limping badly. Mick saw us coming through the gate. He stood outside his shop and said, "Goddamn it, I told you." I shouted at him to leave her alone. Mick told Melody to tie Wink in the barn and told me to call the vet. After the horse vet Vern Aultman finished the checkup, the prognosis was not good. All the tendons and ligaments had been badly pulled, some ripped. He might heal, and he might not. Surgery was possible, but the expense would be astronomical. Not much to do but let him rest in a confined space. No riding. No pasture out with the other horses. Vern packed up his bag.

Mick told Melody not to worry, that Wink would get better. Then he walked Vern out to his rig. Melody and I stayed in the barn, each of us standing with a hand on Wink's sweaty neck. His head drooped from the injection of pain medication. He had cost a small fortune. Margie had said he was too expensive, but Mick had argued Margie into buying him. Melody's dad knew how much she had wanted Wink. Now her mother was going to kill her. I said it wasn't her fault; there was no way she could have known that the steer would break back. "It doesn't matter," she said. She already knew that Wink would never run a barrel or race again.

Frank

I walked in on another fuss. Margie and Melody stood five feet apart in the traditional mother-daughter hands-on-their-hips standoff. Melody didn't want to go back to college. She wanted to spend the winter at the Flying A. The owner, Lowell Hansen, wanted to find another caretaker now that the mountain man was gone. Margie countered that there was no way she would allow Melody to stay up there alone. Melody wasn't going to be alone; Frank was going to stay with her. No. Absolutely not. There was no way that she and Mick would let Melody live with some guy. Melody explained that they were just good friends. That everyone liked Frank. They could team up and make a go of it.

"Now what?" Mick came in wiping his hands on the thighs of his Wranglers.

"Tell her there is no way she is going to live up at the Flying A. It is too remote and isolated."

"Laurie lived there!" Melody said.

Mick looked at me, then at Margie. He understood. He knew why Melody wanted to stay in the high country. "Let her give it a try. If she doesn't make it, she can go to college next year." Margie shook her head and raised her hands like she was shooing away a horde of yellow jackets. "I don't want her shacking up with some guy no matter how much I like him."

We all stared at her. She backed down. "Right. You and Laurie. That's different. Though I don't approve of that, either. Oh, fudge! All I'm good for around here is paying the bills."

Melody and I slipped away to her room at the front of the house. She was jumping with excitement. "Wow! Good old dad. I don't have to go back to Arizona, Miss Laur!" She wanted to try being on her own with a man, to be a mountain woman like me. Like in the Laura Ingalls Wilder books. I tried to tell her it wasn't going to be all candlelight and romance. She didn't know much about being in the backcountry, and Frank didn't know anything at all. But she said they would figure it out. She loved the simple life, the smell of the pines, the mountains. It would be so cozy up there at the lodge. But best of all, she had stood up to her mom. That was a first for her. And she wanted to show her dad that she loved him and the ranch. That she wanted to stay there near her real home.

Mick found us and said to Melody, "Call your boyfriend and tell him he'd better know how to bust butt. It's going to take a hell of a lot of wood to heat that place." He said all of us would go that afternoon to get a load of firewood for the Flying A, then bring a load down to the O Bar Y. Margie was making a picnic. Melody wanted me to go along, but I said I'd stay back and get the house cleaned. Mick wanted to know what was wrong. "My same old complaints. I'm feeling puny again." Partly the truth, but really I had no desire to see the Flying A again, or to dredge up the painful memories of Bill.

We brought the cattle home from the forest in mid-October and shipped the yearlings from the Black Butte corrals. The heifers weighed in at 670 and the steers at 799. Those were good weights, but barely enough income to keep the O Bar Y afloat until spring. Margie made Mick promise that he would keep an eye on Melody. "She'll be fine," he said. "Let her run under her own steam for a while."

The hunters driving in and out of the O Bar Y were making
Mick crazy. The elk were getting slaughtered because of the early
snow, and he was worried about the bulls up on the forest with
"those idiots shooting anything that moves." He rode out in a
storm to search for them and bring them home. Late in the day, I
met Mick hobbling onto the front porch. "The stupid knot-headed
son-of-a-bitch crashed into a boulder while crossing the creek."
The ice had spooked Amigo, and now Mick had a boot full of
blood. We drove straight to town. Doc Johnston patched up the split
and broken toe. "What's with you and your luck?" he asked Mick.

"Guess I ain't got any. Can you give me a prescription for that?"

He wished he could. He told Mick to keep that foot elevated
and iced and get some rest. When Mick crippled out the door the
next morning, I followed, asking him if he remembered what Doc
Johnston had said. "To ice it. There's plenty of that out here. I'll be
back by dark."

I watched him ride away, the falling snow swallowing his sil-
houette. And he continued to ride the next day, and the next. He
trailed in one evening nearly at dark, so exhausted he could hardly
keep his feet when he dismounted. I walked with him out to the
barn to help him unsaddle and asked why he kept being so hard
on himself. He ignored my question. He had run into John Fandek
on the forest. John had shot a cow elk along the river. I stopped
breathing. "Was she crippled?"

"He told me it looked like her hip was broke."

"Did you tell him it was Sassafras?"

"No, that wouldn't have done any good."

"But Mick . . . "

"He didn't know she was your pet. He didn't know her story.
Let it be."

I walked outside and stood in the gathering gloom. Mick turned
Amigo loose and closed the barn door. He came to stand by my
side. He put his arm on my shoulder.

Sassafras had been such a bright spot for me—such a survivor.
"I know it's tough," he said. "But that's the way the world works."

What about the missing bulls? The heavy snow would bring them out of the brush eventually. They'd bring themselves home.

A snowmachine trail expressway developed from the highway to the O Bar Y, past the cow camp, and on up to the Flying A. Melody and Frank came down often to have dinner with us or to watch football and the National Finals Rodeo. Melody and I sequestered ourselves in the kitchen. Things were going all right. Frank was a kick, but a tad weak for the mountain life. Melody thought he missed his girl back home. I didn't know he had another girlfriend. That was fine with Melody. She was not unhappy about it. They goofed around a lot and teased each other, made stumbling attempts at affection, but she didn't know about any kind of commitment. She didn't think he was the one for her. She'd never thought that. She had simply needed someone to be there with her so that her mom and dad wouldn't worry.

"Is this really what it's like to live with a man?" she asked.

"What do you mean?"

"Oh, you know: someone who won't talk to you half the time, who likes making you feel stupid. Someone who never pitches in to do the dishes or the laundry. It seems like he's always pouting about something."

"Do you want to give it up and come back to the O Bar Y? Your dad and I would love to have you stay with us." No. She didn't want to admit defeat. She wanted to stick it out and prove to her mom that she could do something on her own. Plus her dad had paid for a truckload of supplies that she and Frank had bought in Idaho Falls.

The thermometer registered −30 on the day that Mick and I took his old double-track snowmachine into the hills to cut the Christmas tree. Melody left to join Margie in Arizona, and Frank flew off to Washington State. "It sucks," Melody said. "I'd rather be here with you and Dad, but I don't want Mom to be alone, either."

"Do you think Frank will come back?" I asked.

"How do I know? He said he would, but I don't know if I should trust that."

Separations

December storms rolled in one after another, and Mick spent days plowing the road so that Johnny could come in for a short visit. We drove to Jackson Hole to watch him land the plane. When we got back to the ranch, Johnny asked, "What ever happened to the mountain man?" I said I didn't know.

"He's at some place outside of LaBarge," Mick said.

"How do you know that?" I asked.

"Heard it through the sagebrush telegraph," Mick said.

Johnny wondered why Bill would go to LaBarge. Mick guessed it was because the lower altitude and warmer climate of the desert made wintering easier on man and beast.

"Oh, hell, here comes trouble." Mick rose from the table to raise the binoculars. "It's that goddamned realtor. He brought some sorry looky-lou Californicator in here at Thanksgiving, and now he's bringing in another tire-kicker."

The realtor, a boisterous Texan named Mac MacBrayer, introduced his prospective buyer as "a lady from New York." Johnny and I stayed in the dining room while Mick showed them the house and then took them in the truck to see the parts of the ranch that were still accessible by vehicle. After they had gone, I asked Mick what a woman from New York would do with a cattle ranch. "Hell if I know. Mac says she has a ton of money, and these days that's all you need."

Johnny left the same day my parents arrived. They stayed until after the New Year to welcome in 1985, then left just before Melody returned. Frank returned in the middle of the month. "It's like a goddamned revolving door around here," Mick grumbled.

We suffered a long stretch of subzero temperatures: −10, −15, −14, −35, −44, −34, −22. The intense cold created sundogs around the rising sun. I had a run-in with a feisty badger on the road when I skied out to get the mail. I looked for Mick to tell him about it and found him wielding an ax in the corral. The bulls had huge shit-balls frozen to their tails and couldn't stand up. His breath huffed in the icy air as he told me that his Melody had called to tell him that she and Frank had decided to leave the Flying A at the end of February—and Melody Harding had called to chat because the power was off and she couldn't bake her bread. Richard was driving her crazy. Mick asked whether I got anything good in the mail. I laughed: a library book called *No Life for a Lady*! But the good news was that *Friends* magazine had offered to pay me $600 for an article about Mick and his '37 Chevy truck. When he asked what his percentage would be, I told him nothing. I needed every penny I could get, but I promised to bake him cookies and give him kisses.

We argued sweetly about my wanting to have a Super Bowl party. Finally he acquiesced and said I could do whatever I wanted to as long as Old Tom, the Fandeks, the Hardings, the Davises, and Melody and Frank snowmachined in. He was not going to plow the road again.

"Do you want to talk about the ranch?" I asked.

"What about it?"

"Are you keeping it or selling out? Are you and Margie staying married or getting a divorce?"

"What's this all about?" He stopped chopping and cranked on a bull's tail until the pressure wrenched it into standing. It lumbered toward the water tank, squirting a long stream of shit in its wake.

"I don't know. I don't know what I'm supposed to do. I mean, should I start looking for another job?"

"Just stick with me." He started chopping again. Huge frozen flakes of manure sliced off into the sky like clay pigeons.

On the second anniversary of our first kiss, February 11th, I gave Mick a new pocketknife for an early Valentine's Day gift. Melody and Frank brought their calico cat Chica down that evening. The next night Melody came zinging into the yard on her snowmachine with a flashlight in her mouth. I met her outside. "My stupid headlights won't work," she said as she turned off the engine. "Where's Frank?" I asked. Gone. He had left to meet friends at the Rim Station. They would take him to Jackson Hole. Melody had watched his snowmachine taillights disappear. She had considered life alone up at the Flying A for about five minutes before she chickened out.

I was glad to have her back with us and told her to come in and get warm. We would go up in the morning to get her things even if it took a bunch of trips with the snowmachines and sleds. Melody greeted her dad as she shucked off her snowmachine suit.

"The Flying A a closed chapter now?" He swiveled his recliner as he turned from the television set.

"Yes. Sorry about that."

"Not a problem, if you're okay. Are you okay? Need me to go pound on that knot-headed boy?"

"I'm fine. It wasn't his fault."

"Good enough. I guess I'll have to spend the rest of the winter hauling all that wood down here—or should I just say forget it and leave it for the next numbskull who wants to stay up there?"

"Dad."

"Not you, punkin'. I know you did your best. You want to go back to school or stay here? We'll put you to work."

She wanted to stay, at least for now. That was fine. Her old room was still there, clean sheets and all. But three weeks later, Mick agreed to take a restless, depressed, sleeping-most-of-the-day Melody back to Arizona. She said, "I might as well go down and give my mom some grief because I'm not doing anything here except annoy Dad." I agreed that her mom would be glad for the company. Melody doubted that, but said that at least her mom wouldn't bite her head off every time she tried to talk to her. I explained that her dad had a lot on his plate. He was worried about calving and worried about losing the ranch.

"I'm sorry, Miss Laur. I'm sorry about everything."

"Don't be. Just find a way to move on. Figure out what you want to do."

"You know what I want most? To take over the O Bar Y. But they won't let me. You know that, right? I'm a girl. They think I'm irresponsible. They would give it to Johnny in a second, but he doesn't even want it. I want it but can't have it."

During the days that Mick was gone, I read Morris L. West's *Summer of the Red Wolf* and memorized two quotes: "It's only the lies that kill us and only the truth that keeps us alive." And "Someone has to love us enough so we can love ourselves a little."

I was mopping the floor when Mick returned after driving all day and all night to get back home. He lurched in the door to a welcoming committee of barking dogs and a grungy, sweaty gal. He held his arms open. Bleary-eyed and looking like a refugee, he told me that he had "asked the boss for a divorce."

I put down the mop. What had she said? That it would be okay.

Seeing fear in his eyes and smelling fear on his skin, I took him by the hand and led him into the bathroom. I undressed him and then myself. Together we stepped into the warm, soothing spray of the shower.

Tammy

Margie called many times that spring, talking not only to Mick, but also to me. They had to figure out the terms of a divorce settlement, and we still had to find a way to pay the bills and keep the ranch running. Margie thought it ridiculous, but she might have to get a town job to make ends meet. What could she do now? She was in her fifties. I suggested going back to being a secretary, but her skills were rusty and outdated. Would I consider a reduction in monthly pay? Would I work for cattle instead of wages? I didn't know. I really needed the money.

She wanted to know whether I thought Mick would consider selling a portion of the O Bar Y in order to save the rest. The Carneys would be thrilled to have, and could easily afford to buy, the 120 acres on the other side of the river, or the Point. She had other people saying they were interested in the 320 next to the forest lease. I knew what Mick would say but felt she had better ask him. I handed him the phone.

"No," Mick yelled at her. "For the millionth time, no. I am not selling any part of this ranch. If we have to sell out, then we sell the whole goddamned thing and good riddance!"

When he slammed down the receiver, he turned to me and said, "Why doesn't she get that? I have been telling her 'no' to that stupid question for twenty-five years. I am not ever going to be one of those goddamned developers. Cutting up this ranch would be like butchering one of my kids."

The next time she called, Margie said she knew that Mick was opposed to the idea of oil and gas leases, but the immediate income from seismograph testing could keep us afloat until summer. She asked me to see whether I could convince him.

Sick at heart, Mick met the head of the seismic crew, Lyn Wentz, out on the highway and signed a contract to allow them to run big thumper trucks through the ranch to see if any of the readings indicated the presence of gas or oil. Lyn told Mick he had a decent chance. The Carneys had hit a big gas field, and the company was paying them good money to put in a pipeline. In order for the crew to gain access to the lower reaches of the O Bar Y, Mick would need to mark a trail so they could bring in a D-8 cat to plow away the snow. Mick warned them that the ground wouldn't stand up to that kind of heavy weight during the spring thaw. He didn't want them tearing up any land. The crew boss didn't believe him until they had buried enough equipment to build a highway. Mick groused to me that now he had to plow the road and get the idiots unstuck. Later, when he handed me the checks, he said, "Stick this shit money in the bank."

Another bad calving season didn't help Mick's disposition. I kept a daily tally of the calves born and the ones that died. Seeing small frozen bodies bouncing along behind the crawler on the way to the dump became an ordinary occurrence. We nicknamed one cow "Calf-Napper" because she refused to accept the fact that her calf was dead and kept trying to steal every other cow's calf. We had a calf named "Bumpkin" whose mother died of the brisket, but Calf-Napper didn't want him. I spent a lot of time warming milk replacer and feeding Bumpkin four times a day with a bottle. Mick found a young cow mired in a ditch half-dead. He had to put a chain on her and lift her out with the loader. Miraculously, she lived and bore a live calf. My heifer, Little Evalyn, had a heifer calf that I named Lindy, and Big Evalyn had a bull calf that I named Bentley. Within a week, my herd had doubled in size. The O Bar Y calf crop tallied 77 live and 15 dead.

The days unfolded as we ticked off the seasonal work: dragging meadows, picking up dropped twine from the old feedgrounds, tearing out beaver dams, setting head gates and turning on irrigation water. In mid-May, Mick and John Fandek drove to Cheyenne, Wyoming, to buy and trailer home seven two-year-old bulls. The check Mick had to write for them choked me into silence.

Numbers became everything. I counted cows and calves when we fed each day. I drove over to the Bar Cross to help Melody Harding run 188 yearling heifers through for branding. The following week, I helped her ride the Finn place, where we gathered and sorted 813 head of yearlings. How much hay did it take to feed through the winter? How many animal units to an acre of summer pasture? How would Margie juggle the books to get us through one more summer? Would Margie even be coming back to the O Bar Y?

She didn't. She spent her late June birthday and the Fourth of July in the hospital, where she was recuperating from back surgery feeling like a "penned-up old cow." She joked that the good news was that she couldn't travel for months, so Mick and I wouldn't have to worry about her being around.

Melody, however, returned to Wyoming to go to work at the Box R as a wrangler and a housekeeper. It was her first job away from home. When she called, I asked her how it was going. "You mean the mountains, the horses and mules, and cooking outdoors? Or the drinking, the partying, and being OUT OF SCHOOL?"

At the end of June, a crew of fourteen adults and six kids helped us brand, and then we chowed down a big beef roast, homemade rolls, Jell-O salads, and cheesecakes. We hosted a big fish fry over the Fourth of July as a belated birthday celebration for Johnny when he came home with his new girlfriend, Debbie.

Coming into the ranch, with the mountains silhouetted against the sky, they had spotted a mama skunk with her baby, a big herd of antelope, and a cow moose with twins. Debbie commented that the ranch was very beautiful.

"Well, don't go telling that to the gawkers," Mick said, referring to the realtors and their clients. "Let them ask their dumb questions, like 'Are there any fish in the river,' 'Do you get much snow,' and 'Why do you have so many cattle?'" His perfect imitation of their urban voices sent us all into hysterics. But none of us were laughing on the cold, rainy day that Mick and I, Johnny, and Old Tom Astle drove the cattle up on the forest, with Johnny and Old Tom working hard to out-grouse and out-irritate each other. Continued rain in late July and early August kept us from getting started in the hayfields.

Slamming into the house one afternoon, Mick threw down his gloves. "I am sick to death of stupid sons-a-bitches." The nitwit new driver for the fuel company didn't know squat about weight limits. He had broken through the river bridge, the Little Twin Creek bridge, and the Cow Camp bridge before he stopped long enough to assay the damages. The ruined bridges meant that no vehicles could get into or out of the O Bar Y. Mick temporarily patched things with enough plank that we could get the three-wheeler or the motorcycle across in order to get the mail, go for parts, or bring in groceries.

An ornery moose hanging out in the back yard attacked Mick's old cow dog Tammy, who was now stone deaf and mostly blind. We suspected broken ribs and perhaps a punctured lung. For almost a month she languished, unable to eat much or control her bodily functions. I found her in the creek one morning howling and barking in pain, turning in lost circles. I begged Mick to put her down. He couldn't. He didn't have the heart to do it. She was the only one who had ever stuck by him, who had never left him. I said I would take care of her if he told me it was all right with him. He nodded his head "yes" and slipped into his shop.

I carried the .22 down to the water. Taking hold of Tammy's long, tangled, muddy coat, I coaxed her onto the bank. I petted her and praised her. I let the bullet drop her in the sunshine and green grass. Mick buried her in the back yard, picking out a place in the rocks with tears dripping off his mustache.

In mid-September, Margie's brother, John Yates, brought her home to the ranch, since she was still unable to drive. Though it rained non-stop, I threw on a slicker and slogged my way down the road to the bridge to escape the building tension in the house. The atmosphere felt like a keg of dynamite sitting too close to a campfire. The following day, I disappeared into six inches of new snow to stack a couple hundred bales of hay in the cow barn. I saw Melo drive in from the Box R, so I hustled back to the house to say hello to her. She had heard through the grapevine that Bill had been hurt and was in the hospital. Before I could respond, Mick growled, "Now I suppose you'll want to go and be his nurse-maid!" I didn't want to do that, but later I drove into Pinedale to fill out forms to become a substitute teacher at the high school. Then I made my way upcountry to visit Snook and Evalyn, and to stay with Joe and Stella Retel for a few days of peace and calm. A month later, when I sold a steer calf, I banked the money, thinking it might well be the first month's rent on a place in town.

Endings

I focused on hunting season and the fact that I had my first elk license. On opening day, Mick and Old Tom took me up on the forest at dawn, but the snowy hills were already crisscrossed with a multitude of truck and four-wheeler tracks. The icy cold gave way to warm sun, and I sat alone under a big pine tree with one of Mick's rifles across my lap. I never took the safety off, and I never took aim at anything. I simply let my mind wander. Jack Schwabacher had brought a woman named Joan Palmer in to see the O Bar Y. She came back three days in a row and asked all the right questions. She knew land and she knew cattle, and she knew that Jack wouldn't lie to her about the qualities and the difficulties of the Buyer Ranch.

Every time I thought about the fact that she might buy the O Bar Y, bile rose from my stomach to scald my throat. All my attempts to be healthy had vanished over the summer. My head pounded with the same fears that ate away at Mick. Where would we go? What would we do? Margie had a trailer on her ranch in Santa Clarita County and a rental home in Patagonia, Arizona. But what would Mick have, what would I have, if the O Bar Y land and cattle were sold? And why did we have to sell the ranch, anyway? Why couldn't Margie take the property in Arizona and let Mick keep the O Bar Y?

At the end of October, Mick and I went downriver on the trail of fast-moving elk. I spooked them out of the willow brush, and Mick shot a cow for me. As we gutted and quartered her, I commented on the gorgeous day. "Better enjoy it," Mick said as he cut the liver and heart free. "If Miss Fancy Pants doesn't back down, we're out on our ear."

The phone rang on Halloween day. "Joan Palmer," Margie said when she hung up. "She called to say she's not interested in buying the ranch." Mick's face could have won an award for the emotional expression dubbed relief. We would not have to move or try to find another home. We had been given a stay of execution. Mick and I spent the day working on bridge repairs, and that night, to celebrate, Margie and I dressed up for Halloween by teasing our hair, putting on heavy outrageous makeup, and wearing goofy clothes. She thought we might as well try and have some fun. Mick cooked steaks on the grill, and a few cocktails had us all laughing like lunatics, but later, after we had wound down, we sat at the dining room table and tried to talk about the ranch's future. When the phone rang again, we all flinched like we had heard a gunshot.

But it was Johnny saying he was coming home for a visit. That was good. Maybe having Johnny home and Melody close by would help Mick and Margie move forward. I told them that I didn't want to interfere or influence their decisions about their marriage or the ranch, but they both needed to know that I no longer wanted to be a hired hand or the other woman. Mick said again that dividing up a ranch wasn't the same as splitting up Granny's china. I knew that, he had told me that, but I couldn't wait any longer for him to decide what to do. I was thirty-one, and I had been working for Mick for two and a half years. I needed to know if I had a future with him or if I needed to move on.

"She went to town to take the final test to be a substitute teacher," Margie said.

"You what?" Mick demanded.

"Who told you?" I asked Margie.

"Melody Harding."

"Are you going to ditch me, too?" Mick asked.

"No. I mean . . . I don't know what I'm going to do. How can I know that until I know what both of you are doing?"

The silence turned stifling. I told them I would give them some time alone. I moved back out to my little cabin, where I stayed holed up, reading and writing. I tried to convince myself that no matter what they decided, I would be all right in the end. If I had to lose Mick, I would not die. If Mick and I had to lose the O Bar Y, we would survive. If I had to sell Brandy and my few head of cattle, it would break my heart, but it wouldn't kill me. What almost did me in, though, was the strangling thought of living and working in town.

In early November, Johnny took his mother into Pinedale. When they returned, she told Mick that she had seen a lawyer and filed for divorce. She knew he would never do it, so she took the initiative. She had picked irreconcilable differences as the reason. Was that good enough?

The late autumn skies dropped fourteen inches of snow in one night. Margie and Johnny were pacing the living room when I went over to the house for breakfast. Mick told them to stop stewing, that he would get them both out. He left to plow open the road so that Johnny could get his car out to the highway. Later that afternoon, Margie and Johnny left for Denver, where Johnny had a new job waiting for him with Aspen Airways. From there, Margie would fly home to Arizona, disappointed that Melody didn't want to go back with her or return to college. Melody said she would get a job waiting tables or cleaning motel rooms in Pinedale after the Box R hunting season was over. Her long-term goals were focused on riding in the mountains and skiing, but someday she wanted to have a few kids and grow a garden.

Near Thanksgiving I found a wild goose in the creek by the
barn. Injured, it could fly only a short distance. Mick told me to
take it some grain and give it a pile of hay to rest on. I identified
with the lost and injured goose. No mate. No home. Alone and
cold. Hurt and abandoned. I tended to it faithfully every morning
and night. On December 12th, Mick's birthday, the temperature
dipped to −25. When I went to the barn to feed the bulls, I found
feathers scattered around the small pile of hay by the creek surrounded by coyote tracks. Wasn't it plumb dumb to shed tears
when all they did was freeze to my cheeks?

On Christmas night, the moon rose so big and beautiful that
a group of us—Mick, me, Melo, the Fandeks, Chuck and Janet
Davis and their kids—all braved the elements for a trek on snowshoes. The next morning, early, Mick heaved a huge, exasperated
sigh and sat down at the dining room table with a pad of paper
and a pencil. He had to call Margie to discuss the divorce separation agreement. As much as he hated it, he would have to split the
ranch. I didn't think that was fair. Why couldn't he keep the O Bar Y
and let Margie keep the ranch in Arizona? He asked me if I wanted
to argue with her. When I said, "No," he said, "Then you best stay
out of it."

Before the New Year arrived, I received a letter from Mick's
mother, Mary. I had met her only once, but I had spoken to her
on the phone and written to her numerous times. In her cramped,
elderly, but precise handwriting, she politely warned me about
Margie's "mindset about money." She wrote, "Would you please
make sure the Buyer family possessions stay with Mick after the
divorce?" She wrote out a list of antique furniture, heirloom dishes,
and photographs. "Welcome to the family, Laurie. I'm glad Mickey
has you to take care of him. Thank you. With love, Moree. PS: that's
my new nickname, given to me by the great-grandson who can't
pronounce Mary."

When I wrote back to Moree, I told her how much I appreciated
her letter. I understood. I would do my best to protect the Buyer
family belongings. I would try to take care of Mick. I thanked her

for her friendship. I told her that being in communication with her was important to me because it was similar to my love for Mick. It didn't matter in the end how I communicated or loved someone, as long as I did, because without communication, without love, I would die.

Harbingers

As we attempted to embrace 1986, Mick took to the practice of going into a private cave of silence and staying there. The words "divorce" and "selling out" were not part of his vocabulary, so he couldn't deal with the concepts. I often tried to draw him out of his darkness by sharing things I was reading. One evening before he escaped into the auditory and visual turmoil of the television, I asked him to listen to a quote from "The Dreamer" by William Childress because I thought it sounded like him.

> *He spent his childhood hours in a den*
> *Of rushes, watching the grey rain braille*
> *The surface of the river. Concealed*
> *From the outside world, nestled within,*
> *He was safe from parents, God, and eyes*
> *That looked upon him accusingly,*
> *As though to say: Even at your age,*
> *You could do better. His camouflage*
> *Was scant but it served, and at evening,*

When fireflies burned holes into heaven,
He took the path homeward in the dark,
A small Noah, leaving his safe ark.

He grunted and asked me where I came up with such stuff. I was working on an article called "Overcoming Fears" for a women's magazine. "What about this one?" I asked. "It's from Teresa Jordan's book *Cowgirls: Women of the American West*. She says, 'Birth: where out of exquisite pain is born enduring beauty.'" He grunted again and reached for the remote control.

"Mick, once we put the divorce behind us, we can move forward."

"Into what?"

The only time Mick found contentment was when we snuggled together in bed at night. Then he allowed the long hours of work and worries to disappear. He grew fond of whispering in my ear, "This is the best part of the day."

Margie called often. Tension simmered near the boiling point as she and Mick hashed over the difficult details of splitting the ranch as a precursor to a divorce agreement. I still didn't understand why they needed to split the ranch. Margie already had a home, a ranch, cattle and horses, and several vehicles in Arizona. It made sense to me that Mick would therefore get the O Bar Y land, horses, cattle, and equipment. But it wouldn't work that way; it had to be fifty-fifty because they were married. Besides, Margie couldn't make a living on her small ranch.

"Then why does she have it?" I asked Mick.

"Beats me," he said. "I've asked her the same damn thing a hundred times."

But they had the O Bar Y because of the Buyer family, because they had handed down land since the homestead days. Didn't that mean anything? Apparently not. Mick said, "I got screwed by my family when my father died, and now I'll get screwed again. Margie will make sure she gets the gold mine. I'll get the shaft."

It wasn't fair. He was the one who had stayed and kept the ranch going. I pleaded with him to get an attorney. Margie had an attorney. Mick had to get one, too. "And what?" he screamed at me. "Give my whole life's work to some goddamned lawyer? At least this way, the kids will end up with something someday."

"This entire mess is making me crazy," I said.

"Join the club."

The empathy I had harbored for Margie evaporated. Anger on my part grew like thistles on the hardened ground between us. I tried not to get involved in the settlement agreement, but when the paperwork arrived, I read over the pages like an obsessed law student. I marked every bit of unclear language and looked up words in the dictionary. I added up the acres and found that Mick's side of the ranch had a half-section less land than Margie's side. Why did Margie get 320 more acres than him? Because he got the house and barns. But she had a house in Arizona and the trailer on her ranch. Was he going to get part of what was in Arizona?

"I don't get a shittin' thing down there, and I could care less."

But if Margie got everything in Arizona, why was Mick letting her have half of the O Bar Y? The document also said that he had to split the cattle and equipment with her. It wasn't right! "Then you talk to her!" Mick said. "Every time I argue with her about it, she says 'Well, you get Laurie.'"

"That's ridiculous. What have I got to do with any of this?"

His expression said, "You are the reason we are getting a divorce. You are the reason why I'm losing half my ranch and my cattle."

"Mick, that's a crock. The two of you were separated and on the verge of a divorce when you hired me."

"I'll be lucky if I'm left with the hat on my head and a pot to piss in!" Mick slammed the porch door on his way out of the house. The rattling windows and tilted elk head on the wall mirrored his level of frustration and closely held anger.

In early January, we went to town to file the divorce papers and do the grocery shopping. Snow and cold began to claim sick yearlings almost daily. Temperatures dipped to near −30. Mick's old saddle horse, Poco, was failing. Moree was in the hospital. Melo figured out that she was flunking the "life on her own in a small town" class and returned to Arizona. I bought Mick a blood pressure machine for Valentine's Day. The space shuttle exploded. A heifer lost a calf to coyotes. Melo's old barrel horse, Jake, went down with his leg caught in a fence. I self-diagnosed the cause of my poor health as endometriosis. The grader broke down while Mick was plowing snow off the hills for a calving ground.

"What next?" I asked when he came into the house to tell me.

"I don't want to know."

"I saw two killdeer when I skied over to the Black Butte. Aren't they the harbingers of spring?"

"They're lost."

Snook's Birthday

The O Bar Y was known for snow, and during that third winter that I lived with and worked for Mick, the landscape boasted more than three feet on the level by February. On the 12th, a group of us decided to go up to Tosi Creek to celebrate Snook's seventieth birthday. Since the old outfitter lived snowed-in twelve miles off the highway, this was no easy feat. If we wanted to go, that meant snowmobiles. For Mick and me, it also meant getting up extra early to hurry through breakfast, harness and hitch the team, spread hay on the well-packed feedgrounds for the cattle, chop ice off the creek waterholes, come in and change into warmer clothing, and fire up the snowmachines.

Mick rode his little Ski-doo 399, a lightweight go-anywhere, do-anything sled that was perfect for deep snow. I straddled Johnny's Polaris, a souped-up, high-geared racehorse that had won him numerous trophies on flat tracks and hill climbs. No lover of machines, I admitted to being nervous and downright scared. I knew less about snowmobiles than I did about horses. Every time I had been on a snowmachine, I had been bumped off, turned over, or bruised up. I had broken my glasses, gotten buried, and become helplessly stuck. Plus I could never restart the damned things. Even though I had spent the winter, spring, and summer of 1980–81 with Snook on the Moore ranch and I really wanted to see him again, I felt skeptical about heading out. I had never had fun on a motorized sled.

I snugged up the hood on my fur-trimmed parka and tugged wool mitts on over gloves while Mick cranked on the machines. He strapped a big pan of freshly baked dinner rolls on the back of his sled and the largest sour cream chocolate cake I had ever baked on the back of mine. As we climbed on to head out, Mick said, "Feather the throttle, follow my track, lean just enough to keep upright, gas it going up the river bank." And finally, "I don't like the looks of that sky."

A strange sky: gray-green with heavy, ominous clouds. The over-warm air hung still. The first few flakes of snow sifted down as we made our way across the meadows to the river. Mick snaked a rather circuitous route to the Black Butte Ranch, where we were to meet Chuck and Janet. It took me a while to figure out that he was lining up on power poles, stack yards, and fence corners, stable markers that would guide us back if our trail snowed under. We reached the Green and plunged down to the river ice in a swooping roar. I left my heart back up on the high bank. I gassed the Polaris and whipped up over a cornice at the top, crashing hard onto the packed willow-marked trail over which John and Lucy traveled to the Black Butte feedground since John had taken over the elk-feeding job from Mick. Straightening out the machine, I caught my breath and screamed to Mick, "My poor cake!"

When we pulled into a yard filled with barking, leaping dogs at Black Butte, we were met by Chuck and Janet and Old Tom Astle, who had trailered his sled up from Pinedale. With a long way to go, we lined out like a herd of steers headed for water and took off. Janet, knowing my novitiate status, pulled up alongside and hollered, "Just follow me." I trusted her to guide me through eight miles of dips, gullies, and side hills that made up the trail running next to the highway. Then we could turn off the main road and head upcountry.

The next hour passed in a rush and a blur. The men roared ahead, blazing the way, leaving Janet and me to follow at a more placid pace. On occasion, one of them would circle back to check on us. We gave them the "thumbs up" for okay. It grew colder. The sky turned heavier and darker. The steam rolling off the river drifted upward in long, lazy curtains of mist.

We reached Snook's cluster of cabins and barns at the confluence of Tepee and Tosi Creeks in a triumphant arrival. Laughter sparkled around us as we peeled off layers of coats and vests, stacked them on the porch, and pulled off our snowy boots. Forrest and Todd Sterns, two other friends who were already in residence, made room for us. By some small miracle, we squeezed a dozen people into Snook's cozy two-room cabin.

Earlier in the week, Forrest had brought Snook a huge twenty-five-pound turkey. The bird turned out to be too big for the woodstove oven. Undaunted, Snook put the gobbler in a washtub, added some water, covered the whole thing with foil, and steamed it slowly on top of the stove. He made a pan of stuffing out of white bread, milk, eggs, sage, and other spices—a delicious cross between custard and dressing. Rolls and butter accompanied the salads, mashed potatoes, and gravy. The turkey fell off the bones in delectable, mouth-watering strips.

Janet and I had our hands full trying to place seventy tiny candles on the cake. Lighting them all at once became another feat. Everyone sang "Happy Birthday." A gleeful Snook looked happiest when he cut into the chocolate cake piled high with icing. Someone retrieved the ice cream stored in a snowdrift on the cabin roof, and there was cowboy coffee by the pot-full.

The snow had been falling at a steady pace. By the time we washed dishes and fed scraps to the dogs, we all felt the need to get home. The guys circled the machines and got them running smoothly. We called out goodbye over our shoulders and raced off on our back trail. Hours before, the track had been hard-packed and well-marked. Now it was fading fast in the dim, snow-filled light.

We headed right into the heart of the blizzard. Panic raced behind me, gulping the wind of my being the last one in line. I drove far faster than was comfortable, with my thumb frozen to the throttle. If the men were worried about getting out of the backcountry, then I had cause to fret as well.

Snow and ice piled up on my face, crusting over my glasses and melting down into the scarf tied around my mouth and nose. My hands stiffened on the handlebars. I chanted, "Keep going, keep going," like a mantra. When I spotted all the sleds pulled over by Kendall bridge, I let out a huge sigh of relief. As I eased to a stop, Mick came back to see how I was faring. Beyond cold, I couldn't get off the machine. All the others gathered round with suggestions. Mick forced me to walk in circles to revive my circulation. Janet took off my scarf and cleaned my glasses. Everyone else seemed fine. Why was I frozen up like a side of meat hanging in a shed?

"It's that damned low windshield on that racing machine," Tom said. "Here, give her my machine to ride. It'll save her face. It's got hot-grips handlebars."

I would have kissed Tom then and there, but his tough, weathered face was hidden behind a visored helmet. My fingers kneading the warm grips, I thawed out. We drove hard, a frantic race to beat the storm and oncoming darkness. We reached Black Butte as the last pale light faded from the snow-choked sky.

Desperate to Get Home

Chuck and Janet urged us to stay for grilled steaks and a couple of drinks. Mick hesitated, thinking we ought to head on home. Calculating the four miles to go with a marked trail, he decided to stay. After the hard adventure of the day, sitting around warm and relaxed proved a tonic.

We pulled out of Black Butte about nine. As Mick had predicted, the storm had intensified. When we left the shelter of the aspen and pines, the wind sang like a wicked whip. Mick lost the trail. He hollered, "Stop!" His voice was just a whisper that was whisked away. Then he was gone. His headlight and taillight disappeared in the dense snowy darkness. I strained my ears and listened hard. Nothing. I got off my machine to turn my back to the wind and protect my face, and sank waist-deep in soft snow.

"Good God," I prayed. "Where's the trail? Where's Mick?" I had counted into the thousands when I heard the low growl of the little 399 prowling up behind me.

"I found the willow markers," he yelled. "I'll break the trail."

I climbed back on the Polaris, forgot to feather the throttle, and ground the hind end straight down to bare earth. I slung out a string of cuss words that would have shocked my mother and father. Within a moment, Mick returned to curl a circle around me.

"What now?" he asked, as if seeing my machine nose up in the air like a sinking ship wasn't answer enough. He jumped off his 399 and wallowed in the snow before I could say anything. Grabbing a ski, he screamed above the wind to give it a little gas and push at the same time. We made three feet and were stuck again. And again and again. The wind picked up another pitch, swishing the stinging snow in ghostly whorls. Mick's voice grew harsher and louder. I had never heard that tone before. What was that sharp edge cutting into his usually mild demeanor? Then I knew: the hard, tight sound spelled fear.

Again and again we wrestled the Polaris free, only to be bottomed out again. The minutes felt like hours. Sweat soaked through my many layers of clothing. Tears froze on my face. When we finally got my machine up and centered on the 399's narrow trail, Mick headed out again, admonishing, "Stay there— don't move." I concentrated on catching my breath and trying to slow down the dash-after-a-rabbit pace of my heart. We had only made a mile from Black Butte.

Mick reappeared out of the black gloom, his headlight a barely visible beacon in the clouds of blowing snow. "No good," he said. "I can't find the stakes now or feel the trail underneath. We've got to turn back."

Exhausted and bone-deep cold, we pulled into the Black Butte yard, where we could hardly see the bright lights of the house. Chuck met us with a flashlight. Mick said, "Terrible bad on the flats. Can't make it."

"Stay here," Chuck said. "We've got the couch and the floor and plenty of blankets."

"No way," Mick said. "We have to go back now. Tonight. If we don't, we may not make it tomorrow. We'll go round the butte on the highway and head in on the ranch road. It's the only chance."

"Okay," Chuck said. "Call so I know you made it."

The Black Butte drive proved passable because of the trail packed earlier in the day. The highway was newly plowed. Mick told me to keep close to the paved edge on as much snow as possible.

"We're gonna grind off our skegs on this asphalt," he warned. "We're gonna have to really move it to get off the road before the plow comes back by. They'll never see us in this snow. If you hear something come up behind you or see lights, dive off in the ditch."

Rush and roar, eerie and unsettling, sparks flew from the runners on the sleds like fireworks. I kept my thumb tight to the throttle and locked my bleary eyes on Mick's taillight, blindly trusting him to lead me.

Huge berms of old plowed snow marked the O Bar Y road, a canyon-like opening that led toward home. Mick stopped briefly and came back to pat my shoulder.

"Okay?" he asked. "You're gonna have to punch it to get over the drifts. There's no time now to get stuck."

Relieved to be off the dangerous highway, I swallowed and nodded all right. Though I now feared running into a herd of elk or an errant moose, I knew that I could wallow home on foot even if it took me the rest of the night.

Away we rushed with the storm at our backs, hurtling toward the ranch house through four miles of deep drifts and blown-out gullies. Berms of snow rose above our heads like arroyo walls. When we reached the yard, the dogs mauled us, whining, barking, and leaping in mad circles. The single porch light, dim gold but beautiful through the storm, beamed safety. My legs wobbled, quivering like a colt's, as we plowed through the new snow into the warm entryway. Slow-moving, unnerved by our narrow escape, we stripped off soggy, snow-crusted clothes and draped coats, scarves, and gloves on chairs to drip over the steaming fuel-oil heater.

Mick called Chuck to let him know we were home. Feeling safe enough to inquire, I asked Mick, "Were you scared?"

"Damn right," he said. "One of the worst I've ever seen." He pulled me tight to his chest and sighed.

We crawled into bed to thaw out, but neither of us could sleep. The day's adrenaline kept on pumping. We lay awake listening to the storm howl louder and louder through the long night hours.

Blizzard Journal

The next morning I began to keep my journal close at hand. "Weather poor." "The Clydesdales had a tough go." "Snowed again all night." The temperatures for the week before the blizzard were listed at −2, −15, −25, −30, −10, −32, −11. The storm stayed local in scope. In Jackson Hole, seventy-five miles away, nothing but rain. In Pinedale, twenty-two miles away, only rain. We had snow, snow, and more snow . . .

Friday—12 degrees. About a foot of new snow. Got everything fed, used the Clydes. Had elk steaks for dinner, and I cleaned house while Mick worked on his snowmachine.

Saturday—29 degrees. Very warm. Lots of new snow. Okay when we fed the calves and heifers, but when we started down to feed the cows, whew—it was a very tough go, but we made it through. I started shoveling roofs, and Mick used the crawler to bulldoze out bottom bales.

Sunday—23 degrees. Snowed again in the night, and snowed all day as we fed. Very tough on the horses. Had a special dinner of game hens with stuffing and apple pie. Mick said the Clydes

were wearing down, and their weight was against them as they fell
through the packed trails too often and floundered and struggled.
Said we'll start using the lighter-weight blacks, Jack and Jill. We
called Chuck and Janet and John and Lucy morning and night to
make certain everyone had made it home and was safely indoors.

Monday—27 degrees—no power—off at 9:37 A.M. Wind blew
hard all night. Still snowing. Very bad out. Couldn't even get the
blacks out of the yard.

Mick had to get the crawler going and tromp trail and bulldoze
out gates. Didn't get to Mud Creek to feed the stranded cows until
5:30 P.M. No power meant no water, no oven, no lights, no fridge
or freezer. I packed water from Little Twin Creek in five-gallon
buckets for the dishes and to flush toilets. Brought up drinking
water from the artesian wells that fed the stock tanks. Mick
couldn't get in the bottom doors of the horse barn. He climbed
up the wall and crawled into the loft on a drifted high snow bank,
opened the big sliding door from the inside, and shoveled and
shoveled until we could get the harnessed team out to the buried
sled with only the staff sticking out of the deep snow. We made it
out of the corral and about fifty feet before we were hopelessly
stuck, the team up to the tops of their shoulders in snow—and
this on what had been a packed trail the day before.

What wonders the woolly wind does during the night. Just
the top pole of an eight-foot corral showed above the snow line.
We shoveled the horses out, tried again, and made a few more
feet. Oh, the heart they had. They never balked a bit. When Mick
said "giddap," they plunged right in again until they couldn't
move. After a few more tries, we knew they could go no further.
We unhitched and left them steaming and quivering in the barn.
Mick bulldozed and tromped trail for hours until we could hitch
up again. We loaded bales buried under several feet of snow,
which meant shoveling first, then axing apart the frozen ones
on top. We were very careful not to overload. We got the bulls
and calves and heifers in the corrals fed first and then the horse
herd in the hill pasture. It snowed on us the whole time, and we

were soaked from the inside by sweat and from the outside by
wet, wet snow.

Finally, too exhausted to even stumble another step, we pulled
into the horse corral, unhitched, and tied the team in the barn.
When we didn't unharness, I questioned Mick.

"We still have to get down to Mud Creek and feed the cows.
My gut's telling me if we don't get those cows home tonight, we
might lose them altogether. The feed there's nearly gone. If the
snow continues to pile up, they'll be shit out of luck. It's just
something that's got to be done."

We crawled to the house. Stripped off wet clothes. I rustled up
something to eat. We both curled up in the warm sun coming
through the bay window to thaw out. Easing into sleep, I thought
how nice it would be never to have to move a muscle again. Then
Mick shook me awake. The sun was gone below the horizon, and
it was still snowing in the pearl-gray afterglow.

Hitching up again was hard work. My legs felt like lead, and
my fingers wouldn't function. We stayed quiet because it took too
much energy to talk. Mick drove the team to the stack lot and
loaded on just six bales of hay.

"That won't feed a hundred and fifty head," I said.

"It's bait. Just enough to coax them home. I hope."

I rode the sled with Mick and the dogs until the horses, unable
to find the trail in the whiteout, floundered repeatedly for footing.
Thinking I could help by blazing the trail, I took a pitchfork to use
as a prod and plowed the way ahead of the team. When I was knee
deep, I was on the trail. When I sank up to my thighs or waist, I
was off the trail. Slow going, a snail's pace for more than a mile,
but it saved the team.

We found the cows huddled in small bunches along Mud
Creek, only the creek itself was gone, totally buried, with the
water all absorbed by the heavy snow. The willows barely stuck
out of the deep drifts, their tops ragged and chewed where the
cattle had gnawed on them all day. The cows stood there staring;

not one took a single step in our direction. Normally they would have stampeded the sled to get to the hay.

"What's wrong?" I asked Mick. "Why won't they come out?"

"I was afraid of this," he said. "Storm's boogered them. Too many days of snow. They decided to hole up. If they've made up their minds not to move, they'll stay put. Might be impossible to get them to come out or follow us home. One shot is all we've got."

Mick cut the twine on a bale and separated it into flakes that would be easy to carry. "Take one flake at a time. Try to tromp a trail. Go to the closest bunch. See if you can get near enough to give them easy passage. Talk soft. No sudden moves. Be careful."

I wallowed within a stone's throw of the cows and sprinkled the hay bit by bit along the trail going back to the sled. After I finished my first foray, we stood in silence and watched and waited. Waited and prayed. One old sister finally floundered up to the first wisp of hay and licked it up. We held our breath. She came on, one step at a time, sunk belly deep in snow, at times going in over her back. Gradually, the others followed. Mick's relieved breath hissed out at the same time as mine.

"Now," he said, "We've got half a chance."

I headed out on another foray with a flake to a new bunch of cattle. Slowly we coaxed the cows out of their willow hideaways. The herd gathered around the sled fighting for bites of the hay, while the dogs snarled and fought them back.

"Do you have enough *oomph* left to walk home behind the herd so no stragglers get left behind?" Mick asked.

I nodded yes. He turned the team tight and headed back. The last light barely brightened the way. The snow continued to fall with a whispery hush that silenced everything but the creak of the sled and the jingle-ting of the tug chains. Mick and the team disappeared. The cows strung out in a long, long line. At the back of the bunch, I plodded along, done in.

The Storm That Would Not Quit

Wednesday—23 degrees—still no power. Snowed another fifteen inches. We are in trouble. Mick had to bulldoze the gates again by the horse barn just to get the team out. Cattle walking over the fences are mixed up now. Jack and Jill got down in the heifer corral, and the sled came apart. Finished feeding at 5 p.m. I tried to use up the fridge leftovers and dug a snow cave out the back door to put the stuff that needed to stay cold. I never opened the freezer. Glad to have the gas stove and oil heat. Packing water getting tough as the heavy buckets drag in the snow. Like trying to carry sloppy balance bars on an uneven tightwire. Getting chores done and cattle fed takes us all day now, dawn until dark. The cows we brought home from Mud Creek huddle along the tall windbreaks surrounding the calving barn. They have tromped enough snow for us to feed them in a small, tight loop. Each day we try to widen the feedground. It is senseless to put any hay out on the deep snow, as it just gets stomped under and wasted. The cattle will not go to water unless we break a trail for them. That's the toughest part. When I saw them walking over the fences, I yelled to Mick, and he said, "Forget it. Let's just try and get them fed. We'll straighten up the mess later on."

In the afternoon, when we tried turning the team toward the stock tank in the heifer corral, one of the heifers cut right in front of the horses just as they were getting up enough steam to pull the slight grade through chest-deep snow. Mick hollered "whoa" to keep the blacks from running over the poor beast. Then we were stuck again. In the short plunging flurry that followed, the heifer dove off into the deep unpacked snow and disappeared. All we could see was her movement under the snow blanket, which covered her completely. She looked like a submerged submarine plowing through uncharted waters. "Damn her," Mick said. "She'll never make it without suffocating."

We watched without hope, but she wallowed and waded and made a curving arc back to the trail behind the sled, where she stumbled up and fell to her knees heaving, her Hereford hide turned totally white so that she looked like a shaken Charolais.

"Christ," Mick said. "She looks like something out of a crazy cartoon. I hope she doesn't slink her calf."

"Would that cause a miscarriage?"

Mick nodded. "Too much exertion."

We got to the stock tank on foot and shoveled it clear, then made a good wide place for the overflow to drain down through the snow. When we tried to turn the team around, they went off the trail and were stuck fast. We shoveled and shoveled until we dripped sweat and ran out of cuss words. In a last-ditch effort to get out, we pivoted the back of the sled around. The team plunged forward, and we were suddenly in the middle of a big wreck, with Mick screaming "whoa" and the team spooked and shaky. The sled had pulled apart, leaving the rear bunk and bolster jammed in the snow. There was nothing we could do but unhitch and drive the team back to the barn on foot. Mick had to get the snow-cat going and pull the sled back to the shop in pieces. He spent the rest of the afternoon and night working on repairs.

Thursday—15 degrees. No power. Snowed another six inches last night. Drier, finer snow. Colder. Still snowing all day long. No visible trails, but somehow we got all fed by 11:30. Shoveled on top of the roof of the house all afternoon. We could hear the rafters groan when the snow load lifted off. We were shoveling uphill from the top of the roof. We are so tired and worn out. Bone weary. We don't talk anymore. Went out and found the stock tank gone. It was there yesterday. Now disappeared. No tank. No water. Just snow. We walked circles around the pump house downhill to the meadow searching in the waist-deep snow. Mick's prod pole struck metal—a hollow clunk. We shoveled and shoveled and found the tank collapsed, no water except what flowed in a steady stream from the artesian standpipe that vanished into drifts of snow. With a handyman jack and a shovel we worked, clearing the snow from both inside and outside the tank. It was waterlogged snow, and heavy. With the help of some two-by-fours for support against the tank edge and the bottom, we pried the collapsed part up, then wedged the jack against the two opposite sides and pushed the tank back into shape again. It came out pretty battered and off-kilter, but held the inflow water and didn't leak. Mick cut twelve steps down into the front porch, and almost no light filters in through the windows on the house. The whole building has disappeared in the drifts. We went back to work on the roof. All we could do was try to find some footing, hack out a piece of the crusted hard snow, and shove it over the side. With the discarded snow piling up higher than the eaves, it became uphill work. My arms ache so badly they are numb. My hands tingle constantly. At night we are so overtired we cannot sleep. Instead we roll around restlessly, with no way to get warm and no way to ease the pain. One good note: the power came on at 5:30 P.M.

Friday—12 degrees. Snowing again. Two inches last night. Another three or four today. Got the feeding done okay. After dinner, Mick went out to bulldoze out the corral fences to try and keep the cattle in and made another pass through all the gates.

While I cleaned the house and did laundry, Mick tried to snow-machine out for the mail. He came back defeated.

"The snow's way too deep. Fourteen moose are huddled on the road past the bridge. The snow's so deep they couldn't move. There was no way for me to scoot around them with the heavy willows on both sides."

"Are you okay?"

"Fine. But the machine took a hit. When I tried to turn around, one made a dash, ran into me, and dented the side. It sailed over the top to get away."

"I'm glad you didn't get tromped or crushed. I've been keeping track of the snow. I've tallied up seven feet of new snow, more in drifts."

"I know. I've been snowed in plenty of times, but I've never felt buried alive like this. I'm sorry I couldn't get the mail for you."

"That's okay. We've got the telephone."

"For now."

Saturday—15 degrees. Snowing hard and blowing worse. Harnessed up the team but couldn't feed. Too much wind. Came back to the house. Went out again after dinner to try again. Mule had broken down the gate so Mick had to take time to fix that first. Managed to get all fed, but very tough drifting snow and no visibility. Still snowing tonight.

Sunday—25 degrees. Lots more snow in the night. No wind. Thank goodness. Mick had to use the crawler first thing to bulldoze out gates and tromp trails. I got in the team and harnessed up. Fed corral horses and shoveled out barn doors and sled before Mick got back. Finally got all fed and did okay. Got in at 12:30 P.M. Mick worked on the snow-cat all day, while I shoveled on the cookhouse roof. Mick tried again to go for the mail, but the snow-cat blew out four tires, and he had to return on snowshoes.

Monday—31 degrees. Rain in the night. Snow settled about one foot. About eleven feet on the level before the rain came. Feeding went smoothly for a change. We were done by 10:30.

At dinnertime, I found Mick in the shop working on the grader.

"Don't you want to come in and rest?"

"Can't. I have to get this beast running so I can plow out the corrals and punch on the road."

"Can you fix it?"

"Not sure. I'm trying to make a part." He flipped down his goggles and held a piece of metal to a grinding stone. The power went off.

"Well, hell."

"Can I call somebody and order the part for you?"

"I doubt they make it anymore. Besides, it might take weeks to get here. I'll try again later."

We stepped out into brilliant sunshine. The entire world—as far as the eye could see—was eye-blasting white.

"Looks like it's over," he said. "How long has it been?"

"Twelve days."

Spring, Come She Will

The last week of February and the first week of March brought
sunny days and clear, cold nights that froze up the snowpack like
hardened concrete. We could go anywhere on top of the snow
crust, but we had no time for snowmachine joyrides. We still had
work to do: shoveling, bulldozing, building dams to keep the
snowmelt out of the calving barn, problems with the obnoxious
moose holed up in the haystacks. While I shoveled out the door-
ways and washed the windows, I watched a great blue heron fishing
on Little Twin Creek, saw a kingfisher, listened as the returning
geese and sandhill cranes filled the sky with garbling cries.

The yearling steers began to suffer from "water belly," a condi-
tion that caused kidney stones to lodge in their urethras so they
couldn't pee. Mick showed me the simple surgical procedure of
feeling for the stones, cutting through the skin, and then making
a very small slice in the urethra to pop out the obstruction. If all
went well, the urine flooded out, the small wound healed, and the
steer recovered. If not: death row.

Moose overran the haystacks and caused so much damage to the precious feed that Mick called in the game wardens, Jim Straley and Dallas Jenkins. They came out on snowmachines to cover the stacks with orange plastic webbing, which gave the ranch meadows an otherworldly Dreamsicle appearance. The technique worked, but created other casualties. One morning I spotted ten coyotes feeding on a starved calf moose, the ensuing silence so pure that I could hear a bull moose rumbling in the dense willows.

The blizzard left an indelible mark on the land. When the deep snowpack melted, the flooding began. Crystalline lakes appeared in all the meadows. Seeing the fast-rising creeks, Mick drove a vehicle out and parked it high on the hill overlooking the river. I rode out on the tractor with him when he chained a gigantic log to the river bridge in an attempt to keep debris from building up on the pilings. We shielded our eyes from the sun to watch the striking sight of a blond bear splashing across the meadow, then swimming the deep spots until it gained high ground, paused on the sagebrush ridge to shake vigorously, and loped off toward the trees.

The runoff took out the Little Twin Creek bridge and the Cow Camp bridge. Then we lost the railroad car that served as a bridge across Big Twin Creek. The river rose until we could see it clearly from the ranch house. When it rose higher to flow over the end of the bridge in the willow bottoms, our sole entrance and exit to the ranch was blocked. The only way to reach the other side was to use a flat-bottomed boat, which presented a further challenge. Mick and I couldn't paddle in sync no matter how much we cussed at one another. We spun around in desperate circles, slicing rainbows of silt-laden water in the air. He accused me of being a greenhorn, and I accused him of being a landlubber.

That winter and spring left an indelible mark on Mick as well. Whatever enthusiasm he had once harbored to remain on the O Bar Y evaporated under the weight of loss and worry. He spent every spare minute lying on his belly on the 165-foot-long plank bridge across the Green River dragging debris off the groaning, quivering pilings with a fifteen-foot-long hand-forged hook: downed trees, snags, brush, dead animals. We spent evenings trying to figure out how to come up with $10,000 a year to lease Margie's half of the ranch, plus $6,000 for Mick's half of the annual mortgage payment.

I shouldered the bulk of responsibility for all the things Margie had taken care of: insurance papers, bank accounts, bookkeeping, taxes, bills, payroll, and dealing with accountants, agents, and the IRS. I no longer had time for photography and writing. I barely had enough enthusiasm to lick stamps. Because I felt like the underpaid hired help instead of a beloved partner, I nagged Mick to talk to me. I wanted to find some way for us to nurture one another instead of dragging each other down. "Don't badger me," he said. "What's done can't be undone—unless you've got some secret formula." I had traded a tenuous, tough life with Bill for a shaky, difficult life with Mick. Had I jumped off a wobbly raft only to find myself flailing in a river that was surging toward a waterfall? When I told Mick that I needed a more secure future, he said, "If you find out where to buy one of those, let me know."

Margie called often and always wanted to talk. Her warmth and friendliness showed her concern for us, but it upset me and put me at my worst. It didn't feel like jealousy. I didn't know if the emotion was anger or irritation, but it was something I didn't handle well. It concerned me enough that I sought Melody Harding's help. She figured it out instantly: I didn't think Margie had been fair with Mick in the divorce settlement. She advised me to let go of that judgment or it would ruin my relationship with Mick. The only way I could conceive of letting go of my frustration was to pack up Margie's personal belongings and move them over to the cookhouse. I finally took her beautiful portrait down from the wall behind the bed and stored it in the closet.

I countered my increasing ill health and constant fears by walking every evening to Alexowna Hill's grave overlooking the river. She had lived here, too, wrestling with the weather and financial adversity until she and several of her sons died in the flu epidemic in 1918. I squatted near her headstone and talked to her. "How did you do it? How did you not lose heart?" I stayed to listen to a lone sandhill crane gargling away on the feedground. And I heard as well, deep in a corner of my mind, Margie's softly spoken warning of the previous summer: "Someday you'll understand why I had to leave."

One of the draft horses, Donnie, came in one day without his partner Clyde. Mick found him dead out in the west pasture. "Hell of a note," Mick said, "to make it through the whole winter only to die in the spring." He rounded up the other old horses— Poco, Donnie, Dick, and Pasqualie—to take to the auction barn in Idaho Falls. We argued, me desperate to save them from being sold to canners, he desperate to find enough money to buy another team and purchase grain, salt, mineral, vaccine, and other supplies, not to mention groceries. Margie sent a horse trader to pick up Nell and Bell, Keno, Jake, and Smoke. She found a private buyer for the mules Tom and Molly. Melody's ancient Shetland pony Bunny escaped the equine purge by succumbing to a sinkhole and ravens.

Mick's mantra became "I have to stick it out until the ranch sells," because we could no longer afford to stay. His grandparents had passed the land on to his dad, and his parents had passed it on to him, and now he had to hang on long enough to pass something on to Johnny and Melody. There was no way he could default on the loan and lose it all.

More signs of spring appeared: a pair of herons, a flock of geese, a killdeer, two meadowlarks, the first robin, nighthawks, snipe. I walked to the river bridge alone one evening to try and sort out the difficulty of my period being more than a month late. Concern scratched at the door of pretend contentment. Mick didn't want any more children, but if I was pregnant, would I be willing to give up the idea of motherhood, to give up our child? Would he change his mind if I proffered the reality of a "bun in the oven" with the name Little Mickey or Sweet Johanna? Or

would another worry on top of a mountain of stress topple everything? Should I never say a word to anyone, but slip off somewhere
and have an abortion? Or better, perhaps, sneak off in the dead
of night, move someplace new, get a job, and be a single mom?
Possibilities crashed together in my mind like bumper cars.

Days later, when a gush of clotted blood spilled between my
legs, I closed my eyes and raised my face like a supplicant and
whispered a silent thank you despite the fear and pain. Then a
feeling of intense grief suffused me. I would never tell Mick that
I had lost a baby, and I reinforced my resolve to never become
pregnant. Instead, I would funnel all my maternal instincts into
loving Mick, into keeping him happy and helping him achieve his
dreams. And what of my dreams? I didn't know. I would think of
that later, when I had time, when we weren't so immersed in dog-
paddling through the days, trying to keep our heads above water,
attempting to keep the ranch afloat.

Engagement

Mick woke me up. "What?" I asked.

"You have to sit up."

"Why? I'm tired."

"Sit up and look out the window." He helped lever me upright. There, centered in the big picture window, bright against the early winter snow, a beautiful full moon was setting in the sky. Mick kissed me and laid me back down. "Thank you," he said. "Thank you for helping me. For sticking it out."

Somehow we had made it through a summer, a fall, another winter, another spring, another summer, another fall. After meeting and greeting dozens of prospective ranch buyers, an attorney from California named Bill Kellen had put money down to buy the O Bar Y in its entirety for Mick and Margie's asking price of $1.2 million. The closing date had been set for June 1, 1988. I had buried myself in the contract negotiations, working right alongside Bill Kellen and his partner Sonny Peterson, to make certain that all the details were taken care of on Mick's behalf. While the amount of money seemed gigantic to me, I understood that the bank note had to be paid off as well as all other outstanding bills. There would be closing costs to pay, fifty percent of the balance would go to Margie, and then Mick would need to pay for a new piece of land somewhere.

On December 1st, Mick and I got up early to get ready to go to Idaho Falls. The Davises had invited us to accompany them on their annual Christmas shopping trip. The weather was a bit stormy, but not too bad. We met Chuck and Janet at the corrals between the two ranches, and all of us rode together from there in Chuck's super-cab truck. We stopped for coffee and a donut at Alpine, picked up some frozen butchered beef at Ioana, went shopping at the CAL ranch store, had lunch at a place called Jake's, and then headed out to the mall. Janet noticed that Mick was in good spirits for a change. I told her it was because he enjoyed teasing the hell out of Chuck, and Chuck was good at handing it right back. The guys seemed to bring out the best in each other.

The huge shopping center with all the holiday decorations and the crowds of other shoppers prompted me to tell Mick that I felt out of place there. "Country bumpkins come to the city to see the bright lights," he said. The first step onto an escalator proved to be somewhat of a challenge for everyone but Janet. We were giggling like a bunch of teenagers as we tried to exit the moving stairs with grace when Chuck suddenly yelled, "Hey, that thing sucked off my rubber!" I almost died laughing. Janet told him to hush, but he pushed back his black hat and said, "The end of that thing grabbed my overshoe, then swallowed it whole."

"What's the big deal?" Mick said. "You've still got another one!"

"What's that mean? Am I supposed to tiptoe through the cow pies on one leg?"

We couldn't stop laughing. A crowd gathered. A security man began to eye us with suspicion. Mick suggested that we move on before we got arrested for disorderly conduct. Chuck demanded to know whether they could arrest someone for having a run-in with an escalator. As we came abreast of Shubach's jewelry store,

Janet told Mick to take me inside and buy me a ring. He said
okay and took me by the hand. Buying into the joke, I followed
along like a little girl going to look at dolls. We goofed around,
scrutinizing the biggest hunks of rock with the largest price tags,
some of them more than the annual income on the O Bar Y.
Chuck said that Mick might be able to afford a marquis-cut
two-carat set in platinum if he handed over his half of the ranch.
"Might as well, Margie already got the other half," Mick said.

I paused to study a simple gold band set with three diamond
chips priced at $345. Janet said it was pretty. Mick came to stand
beside me. Did I like that one? He would buy it for me for Christmas.
Janet urged me to try it on just for fun. By then, the salesperson was
hovering close enough to hear our conversation. My stomach
churned, and my brain turned to fuzz. All the feeling disappeared
from my arms and legs. I reached out to hold on to the glass
counter so that I wouldn't fall over.

Mick nodded at the saleswoman, and Chuck and Janet disappeared. The little band of gold sat before me on a puffed cushion
of black velvet. Mick picked it up and slipped it on the third finger
of my left hand. He said it fit like it was made for me. I studied the
glimmer of stones on my small, work-hardened hand and tried to
smile. I took off the ring and set it with precise care on its pillow.
The room tilted to spin past me, and all the air evaporated out of
my lungs. I couldn't catch my breath, and a horrible humming
lodged in my ears. I turned and wobbled from the store, found
the first bench, and sat down.

Chuck and Janet stood outside the store trying not to look at
me. Mick came and sat down next to me. He held a small bag, and
I knew the ring was inside. "Are you all right, Gallantry?" he asked.

I tried to say "yes," but the word wouldn't come out of my
throat. Instead I raised my face to his and nodded. Was I sure this
was the ring I wanted? I nodded again. He patted my hand. Finally
I found my voice. "No one ever wanted to buy me a ring before."

"We just changed that, didn't we?"

"Can we afford it?"

"Yes. I put it on the credit card."

I reached out for the bag, but Mick pulled it away.

"Nope," he said. "This is for Christmas. You don't get it until then."

"Mick, I need to tell you something. Something important. I cannot promise that I will never leave you. I did that with Bill, and I couldn't keep that promise, and it nearly killed me. But I will promise you now that if you marry me, I will never sue you in a divorce. I will never force you to give up your land or your cattle for me."

In reply, he reached out and hugged me.

Chuck and Janet acted giddier than we did on the drive back with packages stuffed into every available crevice in the truck. The clock in the kitchen read past midnight when Mick and I walked in the door to an uproarious dog trio. I saw Mick put the small bag in his top dresser drawer. I knew I wasn't supposed to peek, but every morning after he left to harness Jack and Jill, I rushed into the bedroom, where I slid the drawer and took the burgundy-colored ring holder out of the bag. I held my breath and, feeling like Pandora with her forbidden box, lifted the lid just enough to catch a quick glimpse of the golden glimmer inside. Then I quickly put everything back exactly the way I'd found it. I didn't want Mick to catch me snooping, but the joy of the ring sustained me.

We hauled the weaned calves over to the Black Butte. Chuck came and picked up the bulls. The below-zero cold bloodied the noses on the cows we had agreed to winter over. John Fandek brought in the mail, which contained the title commitment papers on the new land. I made Mick a cheesecake and beef roast with mashed potatoes for his birthday.

Christmas Eve brought −25, but my mom and dad drove through a bad blizzard to get to the O Bar Y. The water pipes froze and the power went off, so I steamed the turkey on top of the gas stove. In the evening, with the Christmas tree sparkling and the fire in the fireplace crackling, Mick knelt down next to me with the ring box in his hand and asked me to marry him.

I glanced at my dad. I was thirty-three years old. I no longer needed his permission for anything, but his eyes filled with tears and he nodded. I finally gave Mick a soft but fervent "yes."

"Scared me for a minute there," he said as he struggled to rise.

"Because she took so long to answer?" Mom said.

"No," he said, "because I wasn't sure I could get my feet under me again."

We all laughed, and the slight tension of expectation that had gripped the room eased off into the shadows. Mom asked to see the ring. When I stretched out my arm to show her, it looked like a hand that belonged to someone else. How many years had I longed to be engaged? To be married? I couldn't stop staring at the thin gold band on the third finger of my left hand.

Mom and Dad rushed off right after Christmas to avoid being trapped by another incoming storm. New Year's Eve dawned overcast and chill, with the sun trying to poke through. We received a skiff of snow, but the main blizzard missed the O Bar Y completely. I spent the last day of the year cleaning house and doing laundry. At dusk, I snowshoed to Mud Creek and back.

"Did you see anything?" Mick asked when I returned.

"An otter having a big old time sliding down a snow ramp into the water."

"That's rare," he said.

"And so is tonight."

"Why's that?"

"It's our last New Year's."

"We'll have more on the new place," he said. "From there we can watch the fireworks on the top of Pikes Peak."

"I know, but it won't be the same."

"Nothing ever is. I keep trying to hold back the hands of time, but I never succeed."

Left Behind in the Dust

In March of 1988, Mick spent an entire day plowing a trail with the six-wheel-drive grader over to the Black Butte Ranch. The following morning, in the midst of a cold, wet, and hard-wind bitch of a storm, he led the way with a wagonload of hay, and I brought up the rear of the cowherd riding Brandy. During the five and a half years that I had worked for Mick on the O Bar Y, the 80 original heifers that he had purchased from Ross Calvert had turned into a herd of 150 Hereford-cross cows. Now they were gone. Riding Brandy home in the cold, my fingers froze on the reins, and Mick stayed silent as he drove the team. Selling the cows had wounded him again in some horrible way. He had had to give up half of the O Bar Y in his divorce from Margie, and now he was forced to sell his hard-won cowherd. Though I realized that I was not to blame, that life had given all of us hard choices to make, I wondered whether he would ever forgive me for his losses.

The sale of the cows contained one bright spot during a time of tough transitions. I arranged via phone for a cashier's check in the amount of $129,467.52 to be sent to the Farm Loan Board. What

seemed like an incredible amount of money to me meant that
Mick had finally paid off the ranch after almost thirty years. For
the short remaining time that he had on the O Bar Y, he owned
his land free and clear.

In early June, when the curlews appeared along with the first
ground squirrels, Mick and I met the new owner of the O Bar Y,
Bill Kellen, at the title company office in Pinedale. The months
of contract negotiations and the weeks of drafting and finalizing
the paperwork for the sale of the ranch were done. We had also
approved the deed, mortgage, and promissory note on a piece of
Colorado land, and sent off the certified check to seal that deal.
Mick sat slumped over the table like a zombie and signed every
paper put in front of him. When he scribbled his name for the
last time, he stood up, reached for his hat, and said, "Hell of a
thing when a man signs his own execution papers."

On June 17, 1988, at 7:30 A.M., Mick and I drove out of the
O Bar Y in the Ford truck, pulling an overloaded twenty-one-foot
aluminum horse trailer loaded with fencing supplies, coolers and
boxes of food, two cots, two sleeping bags, a twelve-by-fourteen-
foot wall tent, and a camp stove. Sam whined and cried, barking
and howling from his doghouse in back. I had planned to take
Chica, the calico cat, in a special box that Mick had made for her,
but she turned up missing. Amigo, Brandy, and the black team,
Jack and Jill, would remain on O Bar Y pasture until Mick and I
could fence a 250-acre piece of land with sagebrush pasture, spruce
bogs, aspen groves, and hay meadows where Twelve Mile Creek,
Tumble Creek, and the South Fork of the South Platte River con-
verged in Colorado not far from Fairplay. Johnny followed us in
his 1977 Chevy, pulling the flatbed trailer with the tractor and
post pounder on board.

The evening before, Mick and I had taken off on the motorcycle to see the ranch one last time. We had spotted a bull moose
standing in a pond with his huge horns still in the velvet and a
cow elk crouched down in a grove of aspen, maybe getting ready
to have her calf. We stopped to climb Black Butte to look for shed

elk antlers and to view the entire expanse of the O Bar Y far below. I flushed a hen duck off her nest and saw all the eggs in the down under a fallen tree and wondered what she was doing so far from water. We found a cow elk skull, but no bull elk antlers. A deer crossed our path. We saw a cow moose with her new calf and a pair of red-tailed hawks on their nest. I tried not to think about that. I focused on the months of deadening work just past, the sorting and cleaning, the numerous trips to the dump, the packing and repacking and throwing away.

Five years ago, no one had believed that we—a rancher in his early fifties and a city girl in her late twenties—would make it. But the world's skeptical eye had turned us into a pair welded together by need. How often had Mick and I sung along to "You and me against the world" and "Storms never last, do they baby?"

But had I been a blessing or a curse for a cowman? I gave Mick love and support, gave him someone to lean on, someone he could trust to be there for him when he came in after a long day. But in the end, he lost what he cared about more than anything in the world. He had no choice now but to drive on.

I reminded myself of Mick's history and the way of life that he had inherited. If I clung close to him, maybe my frayed and tattered roots, ripped up so many times over so many years, would find sustenance and the desire to take hold again in Colorado. Mick was returning home, to the county and the town where he had been born and raised, but I once again felt like a stranger in a strange land, a frightened girl child lost in the heart of nowhere.

Mick kept his eyes on the road, and I didn't look back at the old log house hunkered down on the rise above Little Twin Creek or the log barns and sheds crafted with hand tools and hard work half a century before, or the miles and miles of fence we had rebuilt every spring after the deep snows crushed every strand of wire to the ground. I didn't look to either side of the narrow dirt road at the acres of hard-won meadow with irrigation water spilling silver strands across the new grass already half a foot high or the sage-studded pastures, cow-less now.

The pickup and trailer glided across the costly new steel-frame bridge built by the new owner. I didn't glance at the tilting wood piling that gracefully parted the river waters upstream, which was all that remained of the first bridge built to span the Green River. It was over now. Twenty-five years of Mick's life and five of mine vanished, left behind in the dust.

Epilogue

Despite his original plan to do nothing for the rest of his life but ride and hike the Colorado high country, Mick resurrected his great-great-uncle David F. Miller's Colorado brand, the DM, which he insisted stood for "Damn Mean." He mortgaged everything to buy more land, get good heifers and top-notch bulls, and purchase haying equipment. We went on struggling, as ever, to outguess the weather, to make ends meet, and to wrestle with ongoing health problems. We did marry, on July 21, 1989, on my parents' fortieth wedding anniversary, in their back yard in Woodland Park, Colorado.

Margie went on to run cattle under her own brand on the Poco Toro Ranch south of Patagonia, Arizona, and manage her chuck-wagon-cooking business. She eventually married another Wyoming cowboy, Charlie Davis, who loved being her right-hand man until his passing at age 84 in June 2012.

Johnny achieved his dream of becoming a captain for United Airlines and now serves as one of their chief pilots. He and his wife, Mary Ann, and their daughter, Jennifer, live in Elizabeth, Colorado.

Melody married her "best friend," Sy Swyers, but after his untimely death, she remarried an Arizona cowboy with some Wyoming roots, Dan Skiver. She and Dan and their children, Sid Ross and Savanah, run a small ranch and an outfitting business near Nogales, Arizona.

The Fandeks still live on their home place in the Upper Green River Valley, and John still feeds the elk on the Black Butte feedground.

Chuck and Janet Davis worked for the Black Butte Ranch until 1994, when they went their separate ways: Chuck back to Glenrock, where he was from, and Janet to Big Horn, Wyoming, with her new partner, Larry Hegg.

Melody Harding bought an outfit near Hysham, Montana, which she named the Scarlet Hills Ranch. She and her new partner, Bronc Maloney, raise quality cattle and train fine horses.

Bill Atkinson returned to the Upper Green River Valley, bought a piece of land that adjoined the Carney Ranches, and built a log cabin. He still tans buckskin, makes knives, grows a garden, hunts and traps, and creates exquisite artwork on antler ivory.

Old Tom, Snook and Evalyn Moore, Joe and Stella Retel, Ross and Darlene Calvert, and Dr. Johnston have all passed on, as have Amigo and Jack and Jill.

Brandy, bless his champion heart, went south to Arizona with Mick's daughter, Melody, in 2008. At age thirty-five, he now belongs to a young girl in 4-H who rode him in his first parade.

Acknowledgments

The palest ink is better than the best memory.
Wise saying from the Orient

Thus, I am indebted to the young woman I once was for being dedicated to the task of keeping a daily journal.

Many thanks to the original publishers of portions of this work, which appeared in earlier versions in *Western Horseman; Beef; Farm and Ranch Living; Horse and Horseman; Horse and Rider;* the *Pinedale Roundup;* and the *Fence Post.*

Special thanks to all the readers of my memoir *When I Came West* who encouraged me to write this sequel, and to Kathlene Sutton, Jane Lyle, Dale Walker, and Kathleen Kelly, who assisted me with conceptual matters, theme, and tone. A warm embrace, as ever, to my husband, W. C. Jameson, for his never-ending enthusiasm and for being a generous first reader of my work.

This book could not have been written without the support and understanding of Mick's family and friends during our years on the O Bar Y. Personal perception and re-created memories, however, remain my sole responsibility, and I apologize for any inaccuracies.

And finally, I offer my undying affection to and appreciation for Mick (1931–2008), who often appeared to me in spirit as I wrote. He gave me his permission and asked me to tell our story, and so I have.

Laurie Wagner Buyer Jameson
Casita de Luz, Llano, Texas
August 2012

Additional Reading

For more stories and poems about my life with Bill, including the winter we spent with Snook Moore:

When I Came West
Glass-Eyed Paint in the Rain
Braintanning Buckskin: A Lesson for Beginners
Little Dancing Fawn's Tale of Christmas Joy

For more stories and poems about my life with Mick:

Cinch Up Your Saddle . . . and Ride!
Infinite Possibilities: A Haiku Journal
Spring's Edge: A Ranch Wife's Chronicles
Across the High Divide
Side Canyons
Red Colt Canyon
Blue Heron